✓

DREAM POWER

How to Use
Your Night Dreams to
Change Your Life

....

Cynthia Richmond

SIMON & SCHUSTER

New York   London   Sydney   Singapore

SIMON & SCHUSTER
Rockefeller Center
1230 Avenue of the Americas
New York, NY 10020

SIMON & SCHUSTER and colophon are registered trademarks
of Simon & Schuster, Inc.

Designed by Barbara M. Bachman
Manufactured in the United States of America

1   3   5   7   9   10   8   6   4   2

Library of Congress Cataloging-in-Publication Data
Richmond, Cynthia, 1956–
Dream power : how to use your night dreams to change your life /
Cynthia Richmond.
p.   cm.
"Portions . . . were previously published in the author's column,
'In your dreams,' in the Los Angeles times"—T.p. verso.
Includes bibliographical references (p.   ).
1. Dreams.   I. Title.
BF1078.R473 2000
154.6'3—dc21   99-049573
ISBN 0-684-87094-0

Portions of this work were previously published in the author's
column, "In Your Dreams," in the *Los Angeles Times.*

I dedicate this book to four of

the important women in my life:

Both of my grandmothers — Josephine Cowan-Eisman,

who loved exploring the world of dreams, and

Rachel Hoover-Dennis, who gave me the courage

to explore my dreams. My mother,

Patricia Dennis-Eisman, who gave up

many of her own dreams to be

available for the highest calling,

that of parenthood.

And my daughter, Suzanne Richmond,

who is my dream come true.

Acknowledgments

I would like to thank Dr. Steven A. Ross for his consistent support for my work and for me as a growing human being. I am grateful also to Tony Lioce, deputy editor at the *Los Angeles Times*, for helping me to become a better writer and for respecting my work. My deepest appreciation to Pam Easter and Peg Abernathy: I love you both more than words can reflect; you have been the best girlfriends a woman could ask for on this journey. To my former husband, Rick Richmond, thank you for being my partner in raising our terrific daughter. If you weren't such a great dad, I certainly couldn't have completed this work. And my heartfelt gratitude to my father, Ronald Eisman, who taught me to know God and to know that nothing is impossible.

To Melanie Jackson, my literary agent, thank you for seeing the value of this work; I am very grateful to you. To David Rosenthal, for persuading me that Simon & Schuster is the right home for my book, I adore you! To Constance Herndon, my editor, thank you for your patience and for lending your eloquence to my thoughts. To Andrea Au for educating me through this process. And to Joe Parlagreco, who encouraged me to keep writing before I ever had an agent or a publisher, you sustained me with your faith in me. God truly blessed me when he brought you into my life.

To Dr. Bernie Katz, Laura Day, Judy Levy, Venus Ventura, Loren Ruch, Glenn Mehann, Alfred Geller, Liz Sherwin, Carole Coates, Susan Corwin, Tom Chase, Yvonne Velez, Kathleen Murphy, Terry Anzur, Jack Pleasant, Carol Connors, Harvey Keith, and Dr. Jane Greer—I'm grateful that my life has brought me into contact with you.

Special thanks to everyone who has shared their dreams with me over these many years.

Finally, I would like to acknowledge my dear friend and spiritual teacher Reverend Edward Allan Monroe. This book was written in his loving memory.

Contents

✳ ✳

DREAM POWER

Introduction

Welcome to the land of dreams, dream traveler!

Ever since the first person woke up yawning and stretching from his (or her) first sleep, dreams have intrigued humankind. Throughout history, dreams have been believed to be everything from direct communications from the gods to visions of the future, and they have been respected for the important psychological insights they can provide.

Though some insist they never dream, the truth is that everyone dreams every night. In fact, you are capable of dreaming anytime you are asleep but, about every 90 minutes during normal sleep cycles, you enter a rapid eye movement (REM) state during which dreams are especially vivid. Some say that we are actually always dreaming, and, considering the day dreams and fantasy thoughts we have constantly, it may feel that way. However, nocturnal dramas have their own, often symbolic, language. These dreams can last as long as an hour but, sadly, most of these fantastic, often delightful, images are forgotten as soon as we wake up.

Dreams bestow certain wonderful benefits such as stress management, whether we remember them or not. But learning to remember them can help us know ourselves better. Everyone can learn to remember more of their dreams; interpreting their meanings can give us the pulse of our inner health—mental, emotional, and spiritual. Dreams can even offer advice and warnings about our physical health, since our unconscious mind seems to know the status of every cell in our body. Modern sleep and dream research has established beyond a doubt that people need to dream, and that the dream process is essential to life and to health.

Often, our dreaming mind will take a current situation and greatly dramatize it, to be sure we recognize what is really going on in our waking life. Sometimes, through our dreams, we see creative solutions to our problems. "Why don't you sleep on it?" isn't just a bid for time. Taking a dilemma into the dream state can be like brainstorming with a problem-solving think tank. Often, we will wake up with the perfect solution.

Dreams also reflect our anxieties. Common themes, such as being late to take a test, being nude in public, and falling, are related to times in which we feel unprepared, judged, insecure, or out of control in our waking lives.

Many dream experts also believe that about 12 percent of dreams are precognitive—that is, they come true. Biblical history and folklore include many stories of dreams that came true and, today, science has authenticated the same phenomena. Skeptics will write these off to coincidence but, for the dreamers who continue to have these experiences, it is much more than that. Some people see into the future, others have personal visions, and a great many dream of earthquakes, plane crashes, and crimes. Some dream of the locations of missing persons, even when they have no connection to the victim and are hundreds of miles away.

✷

PSYCHOLOGICAL HISTORY
OF DREAMS

Carl Gustav Jung (1875–1961), the Swiss-born psychologist, had an extensive knowledge of the world's religions, mythologies, and various systems of symbols. In his study of dreams, he became convinced that common dream themes run through every culture and have done so throughout the ages. He termed this reservoir of information the *collective unconscious.*

It was Sigmund Freud (1856–1939), however, who began psychology's interest in dreams in 1899 with his book *The Interpretation of Dreams.* Early in his career in Paris, he came to believe that the cause of neuroses was psychological rather than physiological. Later, in Vienna, he worked with psychiatrist Josef Breuer to develop the technique of free association to unearth the roots of neurosis.

We still use free association today to understand our own personal meanings of the symbols in our dreams. Some of Freud's other work is now widely disputed. For instance, he believed that most of the content of our dreams reflects suppressed sexual urges. In today's less inhibited world, many of his theories don't seem appropriate. Still, he described dreams as "the royal road to the unconscious." And modern dream experts are grateful for the importance he gave to dreams as a therapeutic tool.

✳

DREAM WORK TODAY

Some dreams seem trivial. They simply process the events of the day and release them. Most, however, are worthy of interpretation. In my work I have found two main levels of interpretation—the *personal*, which finds a very individual meaning to the dreamer alone, and the *universal*, which reveals universal, spiritual, or expanded meaning. Of course, some dreams can be interpreted in both ways, revealing first a personal message, then a more universal or spiritual one.

Paying attention to your night dreams can help you realize your life dreams and goals. Throughout this book, you will find the real dreams of people who learned about themselves by interpreting their dreams. Using your dreams as tools, you will learn to identify any obstacles to your happiness and fulfillment. And, through your dreams, you can learn to obtain answers to your most perplexing questions. You can actually dream solutions to problems! Some will use their dreams to resolve design or creative issues, finding a plot for a story, for instance, or figuring out a color scheme for the living room. Others will recognize anxiety, depression, or anger they didn't realize they had. Dreams can do all of these things. Learning to remember and interpret them will give you a status report on where you are physically, mentally, spiritually, professionally, and in your relationships. Then, you can use your dreams to explore what you want for your life and how to get there.

So, welcome, dream traveler, to a new world! You will want to pack your journal and a pen for our journey into this enchanted and magical land. Clothing is optional, but comfort is important. No need for a passport—you already have a free pass and can use it every night. *Bon voyage* and sweet dreams!

MAKE THE JOURNEY

*"In our dreams—I know it!—we do make
the journeys we seem to make;
we do see the things we seem to see;
the people, the horses, the cats . . .
are real, not chimeras;
they are living spirits, not shadows;
they are immortal and indestructible.*

—MARK TWAIN
"My Platonic Sweetheart"

Why We Dream

I picked up a newspaper, and turned past the world headlines and local news to my favorite section. There, I saw familiar features: Ann Landers, Dear Abby, the comics—and then I saw my own name! "In Your Dreams," by Cynthia Richmond. I couldn't believe it. I strained to see the print—I wanted to read the column, but the words were a blur.

When I awoke, I still saw the column clearly in my mind's eye. "What a vivid dream," I thought, "so literal and so fabulous!" I had seen four written dreams and my interpretations of them, right there in the newspaper! At the time, I was living on the East Coast and planning to move back to California. I put the dream out of my mind for a time. After I settled into life in Los Angeles, I had the dream again. This time, I woke and it was as if the column hung in the air above my head. I felt compelled to write it down. Now it was tangible, I was actually holding my dream column in my hand! It included four dreams that I had been told by others over the past year. I wrote what I felt the dreams revealed about the dreamers and what insights and advice they offered.

For many years my goal had been to become a writer and author. However, I didn't have a single contact in the print world and had no idea how to get my sample column read by a newspaper decision maker. I sent my column in to one of two major newspapers in this area, and never heard a word back. Still, my dream was so vivid that I felt certain I should try to make it happen. Around that time, a girlfriend called and mentioned that she had just had lunch with an old friend who was an editor at the *Los Angeles Times.* I nearly fell over myself trying to ask her if it would be okay for me to call him. I stuttered. I was embarrassed. Like a lot of people, I am uncomfortable asking for help and I didn't want to offend her either—after all, he was *her* friend.

My friend was so kind and said, "Of course I'll hook you up with him." I was very grateful, but not too surprised—I had already learned that when you are doing what you are supposed to be doing according to your life's purpose, doors are opened for you. So I made the call. Tony Lioce was friendly, warm, and open. But this was a departure for the *Times.* Would people be interested in reading about other people's dreams? We had lunch, discussed the possibilities, and I gave him my sample column. Weeks went by. Every chance I got, I called him. I had never felt so strongly about something. This was meant to be—it had come to me in my dreams, for goodness' sake!

Finally, Tony called. "Cynthia, let's give it a try." This was it! I was so elated! I felt like a kid on Christmas morning when their favorite toy, the one whose name was whispered into Santa Claus's ear, is there under the tree. I hung up the phone and started jumping up and down in my living room. Then I burst into tears—happy, warm, salty, big tears. "Dreams really do come true . . . or am I dreaming right now?"

The reality quickly set in as I immediately began researching and writing. The *Times* ran a small ad asking readers to send in any dream that they would like an expert to interpret. The morning of the first day the box ran, Tony called, "Cynthia, you are jamming up our fax machine! We'll have to get another for the department. Jeez, people really are interested in this dream thing!" We were relieved, amazed, and excited. And we have been going ever since. Now the column runs every week and dreamers from all over the United States send me their dreams. I do my best to help them understand their dreams, and offer advice as to what to do with the information the dream reveals.

My own dream came true and helped me to find my calling, but most dreams speak in a symbolic language and might lead you to ask the question, why do we dream? Well, one reason is certainly to receive direction, inspiration, and encouragement. Can paying attention to your dreams be profitable? Yes. Can dreams help you to understand yourself better? Yes. Can they make you aware of concerns about your relationships? Yes. Can they offer health and other warnings? They can. Can dreams point the way, even illustrating a happy, healthy future for you? Absolutely!

Scientists and other experts have long debated the question of why we dream. We know that everyone dreams every night. Those who feel they do not dream simply do not remember their dreams. In fact, most of us forget most of our dreams. However, everyone remembers at least one dream they have had and everyone can learn to remember more of their dreams.

✳

STRESS MANAGEMENT

The first dreams we have after falling asleep often revolve around the day's events. We go through them, sorting out and discarding things we don't need to remember and gaining insight into those we do. Often, we are inspired with suggestions that we can use to remedy situations that plague us by day. As we progress through the night's dreams, they may take on more fantastic qualities, offering fanciful flights and experiences. Like minivacations, these often-pleasant images can also relieve the stress of the day. The dream we have just before awakening often contains information the subconscious mind wants to make known to the conscious, information that, if remembered, interpreted, and understood, can serve as an important tool in our lives.

SELF-DEFEATING BEHAVIOR

Every one of us acts unconsciously everyday. Some of the things we do are necessary for our survival. You don't usually pay attention to breathing, and if you have an itch on your arm you scratch it without thinking. Some of the things you do automatically and without thinking, though, are self-defeating. Are you consistently late for appointments? Do you have to look for your keys several times a week, just as you are on your way out the door? Do you continue to choose the wrong type of romantic partner? Does something prevent you from opening your heart to love? Do you lose your temper, and later regret it? These are just a few examples of unconscious, self-defeating behaviors that can sabotage us, making it impossible to have the life we want. Everyone wants to be happy, to live a satisfying and fulfilling life, but if you aren't aware of the obstacles to your own happiness, how can you take steps to change these behaviors? Dreams are a way of gaining the self-awareness you need. Once you see the problem, you can take constructive steps toward overcoming these saboteurs. In some cases, you will be able to make these changes yourself. Sometimes, you may feel the need to seek professional assistance. The first step is to know what it is that motivates your behavior, and your dreams can provide this awareness.

Coaches and teachers can help. "You lift your head just before hitting the ball," your golf instructor might tell you. He would be standing apart from you and have the perspective to see this self-defeating behavior. You would be grateful for this insight—after all, you are paying the expert to help your golf game! However, a parent may point out to his or her child, "You are so defensive, I can't talk with you about things." A defensive child may have a hard time accepting this critique and feel resentful. Here is the key. When you are open to seeing the truth and you recognize or accept something, when the light bulb goes off in *your* mind, this seems to be the most effective method for creating change. Good therapy can help you recognize these self-defeating behaviors. In my opinion, everyone would benefit from having a well-trained person to talk with from time to time. How great it would be if every school, company, and family had therapy available, and there was no stigma attached to seeking this kind of guided self-help and if everyone could afford it, but this is not the case in today's world.

Some therapists feel that dreams are their exclusive authority and, indeed, some can and do use dream interpretation as a valuable tool. And, as previously stated, they can be very helpful in increasing your understanding. But people have been dreaming since humankind's beginning, long before the advent of psychology as a respected science and medical modality. So, don't think that you can't learn to understand your own dreams.

✳

BECOMING YOUR TRUE SELF

A bird is born twice, first from its mother within the egg and then from the shell that protects it as it develops and matures. You, too, may have a shell that may shield you from real or imagined pain and danger. It may also prevent you from truly feeling all the joy and beauty, the grace and truth, of life. Imagine that you had an option just before you were born. You could stay in the world you knew: warm, dark, cozy, with all your needs met. Or you could venture out into an unknown. If you knew in advance that the journey out would be at first restricting and possibly painful—if you knew that instead of cozy darkness it would be bright, cold, and glaring— would you have chosen to take the risk? Many would not. Yet look at the world that you live in—the vibrant colors of a flower garden, the fragrance of bread baking in a warm oven, the taste of a hot cup of coffee on a frosty morning, the disappearing barriers when you look deeply into the eyes of the one you love, the adventure of reading a great novel that takes you to places you have never been.

Fill in your own favorite things here, and ask yourself if you wouldn't sign up for a trip to our world if you knew all that it can be?

The unconscious behaviors you engage in every day may be, in part, defined by the shell that you still live within. Until you become aware of your shell, you can't possibly decide if there are things you would like to remove from it. You *can* peck out just as the little bird does. And your dreams can show you the way.

Your dreams can provide you with a gift of vision that allows you to see what your shell is made of, and to see through that shell to the life beyond its restrictions. If you choose to explore the possibilities, you can decide for yourself if this tool is valuable to you. It costs nothing—you already dream every night. You need only decide to spend some time learning to remember, writing down, and interpreting your dreams. You don't even have to do it every day to get the benefit. The more often you do, the more revealing information you will have to work with. The first step to any change is awareness, and this is the gift your dreams offer.

In this way, dreams can help you to become your own therapist. Or, you can take your dreams to a therapist. Either way, understanding your dreams can assist you in recognizing self-defeating behaviors that you can eliminate or replace with self-promoting behaviors. Once freed from these obstacles, you can define and create the life you want.

✳

DREAMS AS INSPIRATION

Some believe there is no value to dreams, but it is wrong to dismiss these nocturnal dramas as irrelevant. There is something to be gained in remembering. We can feel more connected, more complete, and more on track. We can receive inspiration, information, and comfort. Albert Einstein stated that his theory of relativity was inspired by a dream. In fact, he claimed that dreams were responsible for many of his discoveries. Asking why we dream makes as much sense as questioning why we breathe. Dreaming is an integral part of a healthy life. The great news is that this is true whether or not we remember our dreams. Many people report being inspired with a new approach for a problem upon awakening, even though they don't remember the specific dream.

Dreams can also create a bridge between the spiritual and the physical, often giving the dreamer deeper insight, including comforting and life-directing messages. Famed author and television-show creator Steven J. Cannell described the following dream.

My teenaged son had died. It was a very difficult time for all of us. One night, my daughter came into my wife's and my room and said that she had had a dream of her brother. She said that he had taken her up to his new house and that he said he liked it, but they didn't have Coca-Cola there in heaven!

This sweet little dream not only comforted a grieving sister but also made it clear that there were things about physical life that the boy missed. Dreams can be the most gentle, least frightening method of communication between the world of the physical and the world of spirit.

Most religions and philosophies that allow for the existence of the soul tell us that souls existed before bodies, and that they will continue to exist after our bodies no longer breathe. The soul is thought to be a collection of vibrating energy, a culmination of experience and memories that is just as real as our bodies, even though we can't see them. The soul exists and has needs just as the body does. Many believe that while our physical body rests, our soul is free to roam. In this manner, it can connect with and visit that which exists in spirit, and with other souls. For some, this is thought to be as essential for the health of our spirit as sleep is for the physical body.

This may be a new concept for you. To understand it and consider it for yourself, think of it this way. A child goes to school. She is learning but feels restricted by the rules and regulations. "Be here by 8:30 A.M., get this report in on time, raise your hand if you want to speak." All of these things are important, but the child longs for recess. To those observing, the child is an obedient student, but there is a part of her that is able to exist in this restrictive environment because she knows there will be a break, a time she can run and yell and play and visit with friends and quench her thirst with a drink of water.

The time spent on the playground may or may not be relevant to what is being studied inside the classroom. One day, the child may have a thought in this free environment that inspires a project she is working on. She may watch a squirrel collecting acorns and decide to learn more about them. Mostly, though, the value is the contrast and balance of this free-spirited play versus the organized, restricted time spent indoors.

So it may be for the soul while the body is asleep—recess! During this time our souls may visit other souls, check in on loved ones, and receive information or instruction from other spirits. Like a child given the choice of recess and play or school and study, many souls might choose not to have a body and the restrictions that come with it, given a choice. However, the body is a vehicle allowing the soul certain experiences—growth, evolution, maturity, and the ability to help others. Think for a moment of all the physical things that you enjoy—hugs and kisses, Key Lime pie, a wonderful glass of wine.

Many children on the playground might eventually grow tired of all play and desire some structure again. Likewise, it is said that our spirits come willingly back to our bodies after their nightly rendezvous with others souls.

Whether or not you remember your dreams, you may be having these experiences. Sometimes, our dreams feel like a gift—we remember soaring over our neighborhood simply by willing it. We remember fantastic explorations. Listening to lectures with gurus, conversations with world leaders past or present, or fantastic flights of fancy!

I believe that, in the near future, we will see the whole self and treat it accordingly—that medical science will acknowledge the soul as a part of the self that also can be healed. Nothing that affects our physical bodies escapes an effect on the spirit, and dreams provide this bridge. They connect us every night to the other, unseen, but just as important, part of ourselves. Why do we dream? To remember who we are.

How to Remember Your Dreams

A Simple Way to Begin Remembering Your Dreams in Just Two Weeks

Most people who do remember dreams recall those they are having as they wake in the morning. Others, who are restless in the night, will remember the dream they interrupt when they wake at that time. Many people say they remember dreams from weekend naps and vacation sleep more often than sleep that ends with a rude-sounding alarm clock and thoughts of the obligations of the day. Everyone can learn to remember their dreams. This chapter breaks that process down into simple steps. In my classes and workshops, I have never had a student who took more than two weeks, using this technique, to begin remembering their dreams.

Improving Dream Recall

Setting out into the land of dreams requires no preparation—you do it automatically. However, just like taking a vacation to an exotic location, knowing what to expect and planning ahead will make the experience more productive and enjoyable.

First, survey the point of embarkation. Be sure that your bed, pillow, sheets, and blankets are all comfortable and support your body well. Also, be sure your pajamas are not the type that twist or bunch up, making you uncomfortable. Get a little night light, flashlight, or light-up pen for the bedside, so you will be able to see well enough to write without turning on the bright room light. This will help you get back to sleep after writing down a dream in the middle of the night. (It will also be most appreciated if you sleep with someone else.)

Buy a blank book or notebook to use exclusively for recording your dreams. This will help you to organize your dreams and interpretations. It also gives the suggestion to your subconscious mind that you value your dreams. Keep your dream journal and a pen or two next to the bed. If you wake to an alarm clock in the morning, check to see if it has variable settings. Waking gently to music or a soft chime can help you to hold onto your dream. However if you are a heavy sleeper and can't rely on gentle music to wake you, simply give yourself this suggestion: "When my alarm goes off, I will remember my dream." Say it a few times. Just like Pavlov's behavioral work with the dogs and the bell, you will train your mind to remember your dream when you hear the sound of your alarm. You may want to set your alarm clock to go off five to ten minutes earlier than usual, so you will have time to write down your dream and do at least an initial interpretation without feeling pressed for time.

Your room is ready; now let's talk about you, dream adventurer. Ever hear a travel expert say to avoid alcohol while flying to prevent jet lag? The same applies here. Alcohol in moderation is fine, but passing out from overdrinking or drugs won't help you at all. Avoid heavy meals right before bedtime, too, if possible.

Just before getting under the covers, pick up your journal and write down any significant or unusual thing that happened during the day, especially any conflict you are facing. This does two things. First, it helps you get these disturbing thoughts out of your mind—recording them on paper helps you free your mind of these troubles, which could otherwise prolong your ability to get to sleep. Writing this information down also provides helpful clues that may be significant when you interpret your dream tomorrow. Be sure to date the top of the page.

Place the journal and pen within reach and sit quietly for a moment. Repeat to yourself, "I will remember my dreams. My dreams are important to me. When I wake my dreams will flow easily into my conscious awareness." You can use your own words but the gist should be the same. Repeat this gentle direction several times as you lay down and drift off to sleep. Sweet dreams!

Note to the Weary Dream Traveler

In our fast-paced world in which we wake to an alarm clock and jump into the responsibilities of the day, it is easy to see how the subtle images of our dreams can evaporate with the first buzz of the wake-up call. During especially stressful times, you may not recall your dreams, but believe it or not your dreams are helping you to cope with stress.

Aside from exhaustion, there are two other main reasons that we forget our dreams. One is embarassment. We can do all kinds of things in our dreams that we wouldn't do in real life. From violent acts to sexual ones, many dreams are too lurid for people to recall, much less write down or share with someone else. The other reason dreams get lost is that we don't place much importance on them in modern culture. We value productivity and efficiency more than the subtle inner world of our dreams. The good news is that you can learn to remember your nightly dramas without much effort.

EXERCISE FOR BEDTIME

- Create the intention to remember your dreams.
- Check your environment for comfort.
- Check temperature.
- Check alarm clock.
- Check bedclothes and nightwear for comfort.
- Have pens, small flashlight, and journal at bedside.
- Date your journal or notebook page.
- Write down any key events or concerns from the day.
- Repeat to yourself: I will remember my dreams; my dreams are important to me; when my alarm clock goes off, my dream will come vividly to mind; I will be able to write down my dreams; my dreams are important to me.
- Go to sleep.

How to Write Down Your Dreams

Upon Awakening

Whether you wake in the morning or middle of the night, lie still for a few moments and let your dream flow back into your mind. When you remember it, write it down immediately. Don't fool yourself into believing you will remember later. Even the most vivid dreams tend to evaporate quickly if not written down. It is best to record as much detail as you can. Colors, textures, words, numbers, directions, every action, and every person, place and thing—any detail may be significant. However, if it is during the night and you are still half-asleep, try to record the most important facts of the dream—the key players and the main action. This may bring the details to mind in the morning, and will get you back to sleep faster.

Often, a remembered dream fragment will stimulate your memory of the rest of the dream. Some dreamers begin recall with as little as a color or a fragrance. Beginning to record even these small details will train your subconscious mind to hold onto your dream, and deliver it to you as you wake. Don't be too hard on yourself, though. More pressure is not helpful. Simply repeat this process every day. In time, you will be remembering more of your dreams.

If no distinct images come to mind, recall and define the feeling you woke up with. Sometimes, dwelling on the feeling or mood will bring the dream back to mind. An organized and consistent style of writing down your dreams aids in memory and interpretation. It is also very helpful when reviewing your dream journal in search of patterns and serial or recurring dreams.

Before retiring for the night, write the date and events of the day that's just ending. Be sure to include any conflicts or questions you are facing, and anything that was emotionally difficult. Leave room for the title of your dream. Write your dream below the title space. Next, jot down your initial feeling about the dream. Here you may write, "confusing, chaotic," or "sweet and warm," or "seemed important," whatever your overall feeling about the dream may be.

Once you have recorded the dream in your journal, give it a title. Choose something that will immediately bring the dream back to mind for future reference.

EXERCISE UPON AWAKENING

- Lie still when you first wake up.
- Expect your dream to flow into your awareness and become vivid.
- Immediately write down everything you remember in your dream journal.
- If you don't remember the entire dream, write any fragment you do recall.
- If nothing comes to mind, ask yourself what feeling you woke up with and write that down.
- Remind yourself that your dreams are important and that, every day, you will remember more of your dreams.

How to Interpret Your Dreams

T*here are exceptions, but most dreams fall into one* of a few categories. Within those larger categories are an unlimited number of dream themes and subjects. Some dreams apply to more than one category, so look to the predominant aspects of the dream for clues. Major categories include stress-management dreams, recurring dreams, nightmares, healing dreams, precognitive dreams, and dreams of spiritual guidance. (Each of these is described at length in the following chapters.)

BOYFRIEND DREAM

I dreamed I was among the guests at a wedding. It became clear that the person getting married was my long-distance boyfriend of the past two years and he was marrying a girl I had never heard of! He came to me and told me that he loved her as much as he once had loved me.

I woke feeling confused, sad, and wanting to call him. I did call and he was entertaining another girl. He told me that he likes her very much and now wants to see her exclusively. There didn't seem to be any signs of this happening prior to my having the dream.

What category would this dream fall into? A nightmare? No, although the situation is no doubt an emotional nightmare for the dreamer. Nightmares have different elements, often including violent or scary images, and a theme of being chased or put in a dangerous situation. This is a precognitive dream, since the activity depicted in the dream actually came true. Although the dreamer says "there didn't seem to be any signs" of a breakup, still, it is likely that there were certain signs the dreamer chose not to see or consider seriously. A tiny seed of doubt planted in the subconscious may have blossomed into this dream to alert the dreamer and prepare her for the inevitable end of her relationship.

This is also a fairly literal dream. The boyfriend is not getting married to the new woman in reality, but marriage can be symbolic of commitment and exclusivity, which he did want. But, since he *is* with someone else, as depicted in the dream, this dream does not require a deeply symbolic interpretation.

Step One

The first step in understanding your dream is to read what you wrote in your dream journal and determine if there is a simple literal translation. A pregnant woman who dreams of eating meat may literally have a need for more protein. But, if she dreams of eating a giant whale, it would more likely be a symbolic dream depicting discomfort with her increasing size. The majority of dreams are symbolic, but we must first rule out a simple literal meaning.

Step Two

Write down your feelings about the dream. Did the dream leave you feeling anxious, joyful, concerned, serene, or something else? To understand this step, think of watching a movie. You walk out of the theater and, without getting into the plot or the characters or the ending, you have a feeling. The movie may have left you inspired, dissatisfied, angry, or with any number of other feelings. Get in touch with how your dream makes you feel and jot it down. These sentiments are a starting point for interpretation. In the example of a pregnant dreamer with visions of meat, she might wake up hungry or with an increased appetite, craving her favorite protein food. The pregnant dreamer who envisions swallowing a whale could wake up feeling awkward about her newly expanded waistline. Or she could have a particular insecurity as to her attractiveness to her husband. The feelings we have upon awakening from our nocturnal dramas can steer us in the right direction for understanding them.

Step Three

Circle or highlight any words you believe to be symbolic. Keep in mind that the verbs or action in your dream can also be metaphorical. Underline or highlight in another color any words or phrases you find especially important. For each circled word, ask yourself "What does this mean to me?" Often remembering a personal association with the symbol will give you a feeling of recognition, and the meaning of your dream will become clear.

Step Four

If baffled, you may first want to look up any word you believe to be symbolic in a regular dictionary. Sometimes, just becoming familiar with the exact definition of the word will make its meaning clearer. Use the definition to stimulate your own thinking about this symbol. Write your interpretation down in your journal.

Your dreams are your private connection to your subconscious mind and to your spirit. Often, dreams complete a story over several nights. Even seemingly unrelated dreams may be your subconscious mind's way of getting important information through to you. If you don't interpret a dream correctly, or don't remember it, and it contains an important message, you may have another dream communicating the same message in a different way. As your dreams present new images and settings, the meaning can become more clear.

✳

WHAT DOES YOUR DREAM MEAN?

Once you have a dream down on paper, the next step is to understand its meaning. Although the words and images are often familiar, the language of dreams is most often symbolic or metaphorical, not literal. There are no physical laws or rules to obey in the dream world, such as gravity. You can float, walk on a ceiling, even fly, in your dreams. You can become different people or even inanimate objects. At first look, our dreams can seem quite bizarre, but nothing in dreams is weird when you understand the true meanings.

Look for common figures of speech or phrases. The subconscious mind seems to take delight in using humor, metaphor, and slang in making its meaning known. Dreaming of yourself in bed might indicate the thought that you made your bed, now lie in it. Pulling a coin from your nose (paying through the nose) might suggest that something you are involved in comes with a great cost.

Friends and experts can analyze your dreams but, to a certain extent, their interpretation will be a reflection of themselves. Only *you* know what the symbols in your dream represent to you. These are your personal definitions. However, we all share some common experiences, and certain dream elements are what Swiss psychotherapist Carl Jung referred to as archetypes—symbols that seem to have the same or a very similar meaning to all people across all cultures and generations. These symbols show up in what Jung termed level three or *grand dreams,* those having mainly a spiritual or deep meaning, connected to the "collective unconscious." Even archetypes such as the Great Mother will have a personal association as well as a general one. The personal association in this case is based on your own definition of, and relationship with, your mother and motherhood.

In the beginning, write down each word that could be symbolic of something else. Then, write down your associations with this person, object, or action. As you continue this exercise for each symbol over the course of many dreams, the meaning will start to become apparent. Let's interpret a simple dream together to illustrate.

EXERCISE IN UNDERSTANDING

The dreamer is a young woman frustrated with her career situation. She has gone from job to job and was dissatisfied each time. She is considering another change in employment.

I dreamed I was riding in the back of a pick-up truck. We were going downhill and the road was curvy. I saw a beautiful, large, black panther sitting at the end of a driveway in an enclosed property. The fence surrounding the property was ornate, but only about three feet high. The panther easily could have escaped, but seemed content. I felt she was trying to communicate something to me telepathically, and I couldn't stop feeling connected to her even as we drove out of sight.

SYMBOLS: For each of the following, write your own personal associations. What does each word mean to you? If you find it difficult, try defining the word to a Martian—in other words, to someone who has never heard of the item at all.

Here are some of my associations; add your own in the space provided.

Pick-up truck: utility vehicle, work truck, country, farm.

....

....

Passenger: not in control, along for the ride, being carried, where the kids ride, fun.

....

....

Downhill: failing, getting weak, easy, wrong way.

✳

....

....

Curvy road: twists-of-life journey, can't see where you're going or where you've come from, switchbacks.

✳

....

....

Black panther: large, sleek, smart, beautiful, feminine, wisdom, mystery.

✳

....

....

Ornate fence: opulent; wealthy; border, not trap; rich people; property.

✳

....

....

....

Connected feeling: relating to me, deep inner communication, love, desire intent to communicate. What is the message? Am I getting it on a deeper level?

✳

....

....

Using your associations, write your interpretation of the dream here:

✳

....

....

....

Here's my interpretation—did we agree?

The dreamer may feel as though she has no control in her current job. She believes that it is getting her nowhere, and that she is going downhill, or certainly not advancing in her career. She is not using what she has learned in the past and can't see a future (because the curves in the road block her view) with her current company. The panther, content within its beautiful enclosure, symbolizes her inner wisdom and says she should be content to stay at one job, instead of changing jobs frequently in search of advancement. She is being instructed to find a quality company and stay put.

There is more than one way to interpret any dream. Each of us will bring our own frame of reference to our interpretation. When you uncover the right interpretation for you, you will have a feeling of recognition.

Often your dreams will make more sense when you link several together to form a theme. This dream reflects the dreamer's inner turmoil, just as many dreams depict the anxiety the dreamer is feeling at the time.

Dialogue with Your Dream Symbols

When you are feeling blocked emotionally, and find it difficult to get in touch with your own associations with the symbols in your dreams, you have a few options. If, after following the instructions in this chapter, you still don't believe you understand the dream correctly, you may want to share your dream with a friend who knows you well. Perhaps they will hit on something that you hadn't. If you're still stumped, try this technique.

Exercise: Dialogue with Your Dream Symbols

Sit quietly, take a few deep breaths, and close your eyes. Next, bring a dream symbol into your mind's eye. Do this as vividly as possible, using all of your senses. If the symbol is a mountain, in addition to the shape and size of the mountain, imagine what the air smells like on the mountain, what the ground feels like, and what sounds you associate with the mountain.

Next, give the mountain a face and ask it any questions you want the answer to, such as:

- What did you represent in my dream?
- What message do you bring to me?
- What should I know about this dream?

Note any thoughts and feelings you receive in your dream journal.

It may take a little practice but, since the symbol came from your unconscious, the meaning is there also and is available to you. This exercise can also be done when you are lying in bed about to go to sleep.

For clarification you can request another dream featuring the symbol. Just write in your dream journal: "I request another dream about the mountain." Then add, "My dreams are important to me and I will remember my dreams when I wake up."

*

ARCHETYPES

Archetypes, for dream purposes, are symbols that appear in the dreams of people from all cultures and, that have universal meanings, allowing them to be understood by most people in the same way.

When you experience an archetypal dream, you will probably have a profound reaction. These dreams tend to make an impact on us, and have been credited with changing lives. Even though archetypes express commonly understood themes, your personal association with these symbols is still an important part of any interpretation. The following are the major archetypes and their common meanings.

THE WISE OLD MAN (WOMAN): Often appears as a wizard, sage, teacher, father, priest, magician, shaman, or other authority figure. He or she represents wisdom, knowledge, and strength of conviction. When you have a dream that includes the Wise Old Man or Woman, you may be left feeling as though you had been listening to a lecture all night long. You will probably feel as though you now possess important information or understanding that you were not aware of before. Sometimes, the meaning is lost upon awakening, but you may feel that on a deeper level you have filed away the knowledge you need, and that it will be available to you when you need it.

THE TRICKSTER: Appearing as a clown or court jester, this symbol plays sly jokes and malicious tricks, mocking the ego or a pretentious nature. While meddling with and wrecking the goings-on in the dream, it often serves to put us in touch with our *shadow* side, exposing our ulterior motives. I once had a dream where the trickster appeared as a fox in a clown costume.

THE HERO: Coming in to save the day, the hero represents our higher nature, the part of each of us that can rise to the occasion in an emergency. The hero in our dream shows us that we can handle whatever life brings. It can remind us to do the right thing or be the good guy. Often, others observe the actions of the Hero, as such; the example you set to others may be important at this time.

THE PERSONA: Depicts the face we show to the world, the ways we believe others see us, our personality. When it appears in our dreams, the Persona often reminds us that we are not our facades. To recognize the Persona, look for a dream that involves removing make-up, shaving facial hair, or taking off clothing. Make-up and facial hair cover our true self, and can represent a mask or protection from letting others see our true selves; clothing represents the roles we play in our lives. The Persona is the true part of us that is deeper than face value. If you recognize the Persona in a dream, you may need to remind yourself of who you truly are.

THE SHADOW: May appear in dreams as the bad guy or villain, such as the jealous one or the thief. The Shadow contains attributes or characteristics of ourselves we would rather keep hidden, the parts we deny or simply don't acknowledge. These are not usually evil but, rather, uncomfortable qualities that are shown to us in our dreams so that we can become aware of their underlying influence on our waking state. We can't truly know ourselves until we recognize our shadow. (See the exercise on understanding your shadow in Chapter 7.)

THE GREAT MOTHER: Any woman behaving in a maternal way may be an example of the Great Mother. This archetype symbolizes the characteristics of nurturing, fertility, and maternal love; it can also represent the possessive, dominating, seductive, and devouring aspects of the female. From the divine and virginal Mary, the Holy Mother, to the wicked witch of fairy tales, the Great Mother reminds us of birth, creation, gestation, caretaking, control, and, most important, of our relationships with our mothers. This is a common symbol for pregnant women, who often experience anxiety dreams about what type of mother they will make.

THE DIVINE CHILD: Showing itself as a baby or infant, the divine child represents innocence, purity, and the sacred beginnings of life. It reminds us of what is real, what we intended for our lives in the beginning, and how close or far we are from those pure goals. The divine child can appear in your dream when you are in a time of transformation, or a new beginning. A baby can depict the birth of a creative venture, such as a new business or other project.

ANIMA AND ANIMUS: Expressing the idea that each of us, to a certain degree, possess the qualities of the opposite gender, *anima* represents the feminine qualities in a man and *animus* the male characteristics in a woman. In dreams, this aspect shows itself as a beautiful young maiden or noble handsome man. The dreamer who is having difficulty accepting opposite-gender characteristics or who can't easily get in touch with them may have dreams of the anima or animus, which can assist them with this process. If the dreamer rejects opposite gender qualities as a part of themselves, they may come across to others as overly feminine and helpless, or overly macho and ruthless. Obviously, this can inhibit a healthy and balanced life. If this normal part of development is delayed, the person may project this need into a search for the perfect lover to satisfy and balance the qualities unrecognized within the self. What needs to take place is an internal acceptance of these qualities. If a male overly associates with the anima he may exhibit extreme sensitivity or submissiveness, for a woman, this can translate into ruthlessness or an overly confrontational nature. So, if you dream of Athena, Venus, or Julia Roberts—or Apollo, Hercules, or Tom Cruise, as the gender may be—pay attention to how you feel about your opposite gender qualities.

ARCHETYPES ADD IMPORTANCE to our dreams, a feeling that what is depicted in the dream is of major significance to the dreamer. Since ancient times, the cards of the major arcana in the tarot deck have also represented archetypes. Oftentimes, if you recognize an archetype in your dream and associate a meaning with it, it will continue to show up in future dreams when you are in a similar situation or require the same understanding or message. So if for you, the Hero looks like John Travolta, make a note of that in your dream journal, and he most likely will return in your dreams when you need to understand the message the Hero brings.

Archetypes are a link between all peoples and cultures. They demonstrate how similar we all are. When they make an appearance in your dreams, it is likely that the meaning of the dream will be important to you.

DREAMERS OF DREAMS

We are the music-makers,
And we are the dreamers of dreams,
Wandering by lone sea breakers,
And sitting by desolate streams;
World-losers and world-forsakers,
On whom the pale moon gleams:
Yet we are the movers and shakers
Of the world forever, it seems.

—ARTHUR WILLIAM
EDGAR O'SHAUGHNESSY,
"ODE"

Stress Management Through Dreams

O*ne important purpose of our dreams is to help us* come to terms with stressful aspects of our lives. Often, the first dreams we have during a night's sleep concern the factors in our life that cause anxiety or concern. Many of these stress-management dreams are compensatory, helping us to mentally balance what seems unfair in our lives.

Nearly everyone has experienced a sleepless night, and stress is most often the cause. Contrary to what you might think, even good things can cause stress, which is really just the result of changes in our daily patterns. Any change can cause our minds to swim with worry and can result in a sleepless night—or in nightmares when we finally do get to sleep.

Our bodies react the same whether the change is good or bad. Leaving for a long-awaited vacation the next morning, finding out you got the job you wanted, hearing your lover say the words, "I want to spend the rest of my life with you"—or—having a trip canceled, getting fired, or breaking up with your sweetheart, can all cause the same degree of stress.

Our dreams act as a barometer of our emotional health. Often, we are so busy living, we don't take the time we should to analyze the state of our inner lives. When this happens for a period of time, our dreams will show us if we are troubled, and often pinpoint the source of the conflict.

Anger, anxiety, depression, and guilt can all result in sleeplessness or restless sleep. Since each of these is also associated with stress, we will explore them briefly to aid in our understanding of associated dreams.

✳

ANGER

When we feel hurt, we get angry—it's as simple as that. When we feel something has been taken from us—a parking place in a busy shopping mall, credit for a report we did at work, the respect of someone we love, too much money from a repairman—the natural result is anger.

It may surprise you to know that most of us feel anger every day. Most anger is not violent or hard to control. Often, we notice it and take care of it in the moment, as the following story illustrates. Terry had invited her friend Sara to catch a matinee. When she ran into another friend, Susan, she started to invite her but thought better of it. It wouldn't be right to invite someone else with out checking with Sara and, besides, Terry was looking forward to time alone with her friend.

But when Sara and Terry met to drive to the theater, Sara said, "Oh, I invited Diane to meet us there." Terry's initial reaction, which she kept to herself, was anger, and she built a case against Sara. When we are angry we can find all kinds of evidence as to why we are right! As they drove to the movies, however, she realized that through Sara she had met several very nice people, many of whom she had developed friendships with. She knew that Sara had meant no harm and she was able to let her anger go. The good out-weighed the bad.

If it had continued to bother her, the appropriate thing to do would have been to have a conversation with Sara and clear things up. If it did really bother her and she *didn't* bring it up, the anger would have been added to her anger vault and could easily come out later. When this happens, the anger is not always unleashed on the person who contributed to these feelings. Often, it is directed at a close friend or family member with whom the angry person feels safe. Nearly everyone has been the recipient of this type of lashing out. When it happens to us, we wonder, "What got you going?" The other person may not realize in the moment how inappropriate and over the top their reaction is. Handled this way, the anger becomes destructive and will result in many problems, not the least being sleepless nights and unsettling dreams.

What you do with the feeling of anger is the key to avoiding sleeplessness and unsettling dreams. Many of us, especially fe-males, were taught that it is not okay to be angry. "It isn't pretty, it isn't nice, just let it go!"

If we hold anger in or try to let it go without working with it and coming to a resolution, the anger will collect deep inside our psyches. It is as though there is a big vault for storing anger and the reserves just keep getting bigger until the vault is bulging. When the door can no longer close and lock, some of it has to seep out, and it will usually pick the most inopportune moment to do that! If you are not comfortable expressing your anger in constructive ways, the anger will then be forced to be released through your dream state. You may think that you have let it all go, but you can't fool your subconscious.

Another suggestion to help you process your anger is to keep a journal. You might even write with a red pen, since red is associated with anger. Write about your angry feelings, and keep writing until you feel relieved. Often, getting it out of your system in this manner is very therapeutic. Once they are recorded on paper, you can re-lease the angry thoughts from your mind and calm down. Often, in reading back what you've written, the entire situation that had your blood boiling moments or days before can seems trivial or less important.

※

ANXIETY

Many dreams reflect anxiety, another type of stress. Anxiety is an anticipation of the future and, most often, fear of the outcome of future events—even those ten minutes in the future. People who suffer from anxiety worry about being hurt or losing something important. Fear serves an important purpose, causing us to be on the alert, to protect or defend ourselves. Irrational fears and phobias can also cause anxiety.

The classic dream of arriving on campus and not being able to find your classroom, or having to take a test you haven't studied for are anxiety dreams. They can come anytime you feel that you are not prepared, or that you will be tested or judged and may not live up to expectations. If these dreams result in extra study or preparation on your part, they can be helpful. If you are truly ready for what is ahead, your dreams may be based on something from the past. In this case, take a break from study or preparation and try to relax. Some people are just poor test takers, even though they know the information that will be covered. To avoid anxiety dreams, pinpoint your exact fears and face them. If you fear for your safety, for example, you may want to take a self-defense course. If you fear speaking at a company conference, take a public-speaking course and rehearse until the speech comes easily.

※

RUTH'S DREAM

I dreamed I answered the door bell and, there on the porch was a darling, little, white, fluffy dog; it was so cute. My son was behind me looking over my right shoulder. I let the puppy walk into my home, but as it did it turned into a pig! A black-and-white pig. I was mortified and didn't want it in my home.

I asked Ruth if her life may have contained a similar situation—in which something started out looking cute but changed into something else once it came into her home or her life. Perhaps something mortifying that made her question letting it into her life in the first place.

Ruth's eyes lit up in recognition. She was concerned about her adult son. He was in a romantic relationship with a woman whom Ruth said had started out sweet. She had been happy that her son had companionship and had encouraged the relationship, and invited the couple over for dinner. In recent weeks, however, the new girlfriend had borrowed and crashed her son's car and had acted very cruelly toward him. Ruth suspected drug use, saying she saw all the symptoms, and was concerned that the girlfriend could become violent with her son. She wasn't sure how to handle the situation. She also felt angry with herself for not being a better judge of character.

Ruth's dream did indicate that she had been deceived. Once she had accepted into her life the white (pure, truthful) puppy (friendly, cute), it changed into a pig (greedy, dirty); the black and white colors represent the polarity of good and evil. Her son behind her, protected by her and over her right shoulder, indicates that Ruth shoulders some responsibility for protecting her son.

After having this dream, Ruth decided to admit her concern to her son and offer to help him get the woman out of his life. As many parents of adult children understand, this type of situation can be very delicate, and must be handled carefully. Ruth was able to gently point out her concerns to her son and when he eventually was able to see his girlfriend's deceit, he made the choice to end the destructive relationship.

※

Depression

Depression can also be filed under the label *stress.* Depression, in a sense, is the opposite of anxiety in that it involves fear of the past. Rehashing past decisions and circumstances can lead to depression. Everyone feels sad from time to time—many things touch our hearts with sadness in this life—but sadness should heal as you move on with your daily life and experience the good that surrounds you. If you dwell on what is wrong, on your losses and, perhaps, poor choices in the past, depression can result.

A distinction must be made between clinical depression and sadness. Symptoms of the former often include one or more of the following: a loss of appetite, change in sleeping patterns, either much more sleep or practically none, a loss of desire for sex, and, in fact, a loss of interest in anything that previously brought pleasure. There is often an accompanying feeling of hopelessness. Patients with depression describe this feeling as "no light at the end of the tunnel." If you recognize any of the symptoms of clinical depression, there is marvelous help available. Many patients respond well to cognitive therapy while others require some medication to help balance their brain chemistry. Often, combining both of these modalities is most effective. Don't delay in reaching for help. Your physician can be the best source for assistance. Depression is treatable and you can return to a fulfilling and satisfying life.

Depression often involves anger directed at the self. If you have buried these feelings or are not consciously aware of them, they may display themselves in your dreams. Often, these dreams involve critical self-judgment and a feeling of being trapped.

One example of a depression-rooted dream comes from Harold, in his late eighties. He lived in a convalescent home. His wife had passed on years before; his children lived elsewhere and didn't visit often. Harold's interest in life was scant—he didn't even shave himself anymore. Not that he wasn't capable of simple grooming tasks; it was just that there was no one to get spiffed up for anymore.

Harold was always tired, but hated going to sleep because he had terrible dreams. He didn't want any reruns of these nightmares. In his dreams, almost nightly, Harold was kicked, hit, and beaten by others. Sometimes the beaters were faceless strangers but, other times, they were his four sons. If you asked Harold he would say he had been a strict father, preparing his boys to be tough in a tougher world. If you asked his sons, they would say he had been cruel, physically and emotionally. The sons have the scars to prove it.

Years of pushing down and rationalizing the truth exploded in nightly nightmares once Harold stopped living an active life. Harold never acknowledged the feelings of his sons and he died a depressed, mentally tortured man.

Our minds are powerful. We can override a lot when necessary for survival but, sooner or later, we will have to face what we hold in. To avoid depressing dreams, do your best to face the truth and make amends or heal whatever you can. We can only live in the moment, but it is never too late to acknowledge the past and, where necessary, heal our relationships with others and forgive ourselves.

*

GUILT

Guilt can result from the anger you hold inside if you allow it to turn against yourself. Guilt involves feeling bad, unworthy, or remorseful, and it can lead to self-hatred. As with all of these stressful feelings, it is appropriate at times. If you are responsible for doing wrong, you should feel guilty. Feeling guilty should then propel you to do the right thing. Once the corrective action is taken the guilt should go away. You may think that your feelings about past actions are resolved, but your dreams reveal otherwise.

Mirian is an attractive, single woman in her early forties. She has never been married, but would love to marry and have children. She has had four opportunities to get married. Each time the man was a nice and good person. And, each time, Mirian had loving feelings for the man, but she found a reason to decline each proposal. One man wasn't attractive enough, even though he adored her and they had fun together. Another was too short. One was too smart and the other was employed in a profession Mirian didn't feel was exciting. Mirian believed that each rejection was the right thing to do at the time—after all, she had her ideal list of traits and characteristics and she did not want to settle. The truth is that, from time to time, when Mirian allows herself to remember her past, she feels remorse. It has been several years since she has dated someone who interested her. She second-guesses herself. Maybe she was too superficial in the past. Maybe she will never get another chance. Maybe she was secretly afraid of being a wife.

She rarely talks about this part of her past even with her closest friends and family, even though her mother frequently tries to bring up the subject. Mirian is tormented by dreams of being left at the altar. She dreams about the men she has loved and sees them happily married to others. In her worst nightmare, she dreams of the children she would have given birth to and the family vacations she would have taken. She wakes in a pool of sweat. She feels guilty and alone. Guilt can be a living hell.

AS DEBILITATING AS stress can be, you do have options for overcoming it. One is to keep a journal of your dreams and your feelings. Becoming aware of them in this fashion can help you to take the appropriate action to clean up and heal these situations. It may also be very helpful to seek professional counseling. Trained mental-health care therapists can be instrumental in helping you process the cause of stress, and restoring a sense of well-being will lighten your dream life as well as your waking state.

Recurring Dreams

Recurring dreams are urgent messages from your unconscious mind. Like nagging children who won't stop calling your name until you acknowledge them, recurring dreams demand to be understood. They will repeat until you gain conscious awareness of the message they send. Often these dreams change slightly each time you have them, and that subtle difference may be an important clue as to their meaning. Sometimes the theme is repeated and not the specific dream. If a recurring dream is not understood after several tries, your unconscious mind will often compose another dream story that will convey the same message. Once understood, the dream may come back when you are in a similar situation in the future.

GRACE'S STORY

I was in a bad relationship, but it started off so great. I felt so loved and honored. We met about a year after my divorce. I had been depressed, but when I met Earl he made me feel beautiful. I thought the universe was rewarding me for all the turmoil I had been through by bringing this loving man into my life. After a few months, he started taking away all the compliments and loving behavior. He really changed. He talked a lot about his past relationship. I felt that he still had feelings for his ex, but he talked about her in a very negative way. He grew moody. He could be very verbally abusive. We would have a bad day, but then we would have a good day, laughing and playing. I was so confused. I felt like I was on a roller coaster and I couldn't get off. I tried to be patient and helpful. I loved him so much. I didn't know what to do. And then I began having these dreams.

I dreamed about bathrooms. That was the common theme. I needed to find a bathroom. The need was urgent. Sometimes I would go through a maze, finally thinking I had found the toilet stall but, when I opened the door, it was just a dressing room with no toilet. Or the toilet would be filthy, or it would be a primitive floor-sink-type bathroom like I had seen in Asia. Time after time I had these bathroom dreams.

Grace's recurring theme was a strong warning. Bathrooms represent cleansing, and toilets are where we let go and release what is no longer of benefit to us. With Earl, it was time for her to let go, but she was having a hard time finding the way to do that. She didn't want to release something that could be repaired. She didn't want to fail in another relationship, but her unconscious mind was telling her that she needed to let go. The more she held on, the more distressed she became. Once Grace told Earl that she needed to break up with him, and he accepted this, the toilet dreams stopped.

Recurring dreams are a gift. Huge life lessons can be understood when we take these repeated visions seriously.

ANDRE IS CHASED BY A DEVIL

Andre is a teenaged boy who balances school, a part-time job, his family, and a social life.

I have had this dream for at least five years now. I have wings like an angel and I am flying through the sky when a flying red devil starts chasing me. The devil gets closer and closer, gaining on me. I worry about what will happen when he finally catches up to me.

This is a dream depicting the human conflict between good and evil. Andre sees himself as good, free to fly or proceed with his life unobstructed. Flying in the sky, it seems there are no limits to what he can achieve, but the flying devil represents temptation and evil. We are all constantly put in the position of deciding for ourselves how we will deal with temptation. Sometimes we are a little tempted to do something we later might feel bad about (in Andre's dream this may be when the devil gets close.) However, temptation and evil serve an important purpose in our lives, forcing us to define ourselves by rejecting them. Making the right choices helps you feel good about yourself, thus creating confidence and self-esteem. As long as Andre continues to have this dream, he may feel a little insecure about whether he will be able to resist the temptation that, at times, hovers near. Asking, "What do I find tempting or threatening?" and "How can I reinforce my commitment to what is right?" could shed light on any insecurity and help Andre squelch that flying devil.

JENNY'S BIRDCAGE

Jenny is a busy woman in her thirties. She has many responsibilities and is up for a promotion. Her job is not her dream career, but she does hope to get the advancement. Still, her boss heaps extra duties on her and she wonders when she will have time for a vacation—or a date, for that matter.

In my recurring dream, the details vary but the gist is the same. I come across a birdcage with a bird I have forgotten to feed. I never seem to get around to feeding this bird as I can't find any food. Then my dream goes on to something else.

Jenny's personal associations with particular sorts of birds may color her dream but, generally, birds, since they can fly, represent freedom. A pet represents a living thing within our care and responsibility. The cage represents being cooped up, a loss of freedom, but it is also a trap we can see through. Food, of course, is required to sustain life and is symbolic of nurturing, love, and spiritual sustenance. So this dream suggests that Jenny is not nurturing her free will. She feels as though a part of her is locked up, unable to express itself. She may not believe that she has access to the nurturing and support she needs. Her dream is a call to empower herself and take control of her life. Asking questions such as, "Where in my life do I feel trapped?" and "What would I need to feel nurtured and supported?" could reveal areas to work on.

MICHAEL'S DREAM TOOK TWENTY-FIVE YEARS TO UNRAVEL, BUT IT MADE HIM RICH AND CHANGED THE WORLD

Michael Barnsley was a good student and especially fond of math and science. At age fifteen, he found the English boarding school he attended fascinating and, at times, challenging. One particular night after studying for a math exam Michael went to sleep and had a dream.

I dreamed of an old-fashioned telephone switchboard. The cables were all tangled up and crossed. They resembled a plate of spaghetti; there was no order at all.

Michael continued to have this same baffling dream sporadically for the next twenty-five years! He assumed it had meaning, but was at a loss as to what it could be. He went on to become a professor and mathematician and found himself trying to resolve a particular dilemma: Could someone develop a mathematical formula to define and reproduce any picture? Geometric images were one thing, but what about random shapes such as the contour of a leaf: Could one create a formula to duplicate it exactly every time?

On the morning of March 26, 1988, Michael woke and knew his life would never be the same again. He had had the dream again . . . but this time the cords were all untangled. The night before, he had spent time looking at a painting his recently deceased father had left for him. (Interestingly, March 26 was Michael's father's birthday.) The painting depicted an image of a window frame within which was another, the pattern repeating deeper and deeper in perspective into the canvas.

The image in the painting inspired the untangling of the dream and the creation of fractals. *Fractals* break pictures into digital lines rather than the dots or pixels computer technology had used in the years prior. Essentially, fractals are a frame within a frame. Fractals allow a much more realistic and accurate presentation than former technology allowed, even in dramatically enlarged images. Michael started a company with an associate; they called it Iterated Systems. They were able to develop this new method into a technology that is now widely used in computer programs. In fact, Microsoft used the technology in the first CD-ROM encyclopedia ever created. Today, Michael remains on the board of Iterated Systems, but he sold the company and lives very comfortably on the profits of a dream.

WRITING YOUR DREAMS down each morning will help you to keep track of the recurring dreams and dream themes you experience. Spending time to unravel their mystery can provide the keys you need to create the life you want. The meaning of a recurring dream can become your personal mission statement.

Nightmares

Nightmares provide valuable insights into some of the deeper chambers of our psyche. All dreams, even nightmares, can be positive and helpful once they are understood.

Everyone has experienced a nightmare at some time. Some people have them frequently. They stand apart from our other dreams because of their vivid, scary, threatening, and/or violent images. Often, people who do not remember the majority of their nightly dreams will remember their nightmares.

In the past, nightmares were thought to be delivered by evil spirits as a form of punishment, the helpless sleeper "attacked" by the frightening images. Often, the inspiration for the attack is guilt, a self-attack to balance a transgression. Oftentimes dreamers feel as if they are being suffocated. Many plays and operas depict scenes in which dreams motivate someone to right a wrong. Consider Scrooge in *A Christmas Carol.* Visited by ghosts in his dreams, he recognizes that his miserly treatment of others will lead him to a terrible afterlife. He wakes from his dream ready to make amends and change his ways.

Nightmares serve an important purpose. They show us what is troubling us on deep levels, things we may not be aware of in our waking state. The more horrifying the dream is, the more likely we are to remember it, and the more important it is to take time to understand it. In this sense, nightmares can be considered an endowment from our unconscious mind; they point out what is really bothering us. It is important to understand the meaning, so that we can address these frustrations, fears, anxieties, inner conflicts, or depressions and relieve our psychic stress. Often, because of our survival instincts, we push down distressing feelings and try to just get over it. If we haven't resolved the source of the problem it will eventually resurface from our inner depths to be dealt with. Nightmares get our attention! You may continue to have these vivid and or scary images until you resolve the problem, or your unconscious may try a different dream scenario to convey the same message. The following dream illustrates how powerful a nightmare's message can be.

I am being chased by flesh-eating zombies. They always find me; there is no place to hide. The zombies are right at my heels and though they never actually get me, they are always very close. I cry, shout, and fight during these recurring nightmares and have to be physically woken up to feel released.

This dreamer was involved in a very abusive marriage while having this dream. Clearly, she felt threatened and as though she could be eaten alive. The zombies could represent her abusive spouse, an unfeeling and frightening being. The zombies *could* also represent her. A zombie is a corpse that moves in a trancelike, mechanical way. This dreamer may have felt dead inside, only going through the motions of daily living. Her dream finally helped her to realize that if she didn't get the courage to leave this abusive situation, she might as well be dead.

PURSUIT DREAMS

One common nightmare involves being chased; sometimes we are being pursued by a monster, sometimes by an unknown villain. In some dreams we run and run and try to outsmart the pursuer by hiding. In others, we feel paralyzed and can't get away. Chase dreams can also indicate that we feel pursued by an addiction, deadline, or other pressures.

Often I have waking dreams in which I feel helplessly caught in between being awake and being in the actual dream state. There is a very real sense of impending danger and peril and an inability to react. This brings on seizurelike paralysis. The struggle to break free from the cusp of the dream state and paralysis, and get back to reality so I can react, always requires a conscious, maddening effort.

Many who experience nightmares share this same scary inability to shake off the sleep or dream state and react. During *rapid eye movement,* or REM sleep, the major muscles of the body are effectively paralyzed. This is thought to be a natural mechanism to prevent the body from injuring itself during violent or active dreams. It can be very frustrating since, for a few moments, the body is still in the sleep state while the mind is awake and struggling to take action. You can't stop this from occurring, but knowing that it is normal and that you will soon be fully awake and able to move as you wish should relieve the frustration.

There may also be another explanation for these paralyzed states. For those who believe that the spirit is free to explore while the body is resting each night, this feeling of being paralyzed may accompany the period when the spirit is re-entering the physical body. Just before the spirit returns home, the dreamer may be aware on many levels at the same time, feeling the body, which is in the sleep-paralysis state, and the spirit returning from a dream exploration. This might feel like a vulnerable situation, and explain the panic some feel.

✳

WHEN YOU ARE THE BAD GUY

Another type of nightmare depicts the dreamer herself as the villain. Remember that everyone in your dream might be an aspect of yourself, so you may be running from some dark or scary part of you. Dreams can grow out of envy, guilt, anger, or other suppressed emotions or characteristics. Being willing to take a perceptive look into certain dark or shadowy aspects of self can relieve this pressure. We all have a dark side, and our willingness to accept and understand this part will go a long way toward helping balance our mental health.

To gain awareness of your shadow side and, perhaps, increase your understanding of your nightmares, try this exercise:

On the left side of a piece of paper, make a list of ten positive words or phrases that describe you. Examples could include patient, good listener, friendly, well organized, smart, compassionate, good cook, dedicated parent, attractive, good friend. Then, across from each of these words or phrases write the equivalent opposite word or phrase. In our example these might be: impatient, bad listener, unfriendly, disorganized, uncaring, bad cook, neglectful parent, unattractive, bad friend.

Now take your list to the mirror. Try saying "I am," and then inserting each of the negative words or phrases. Which words are easy to accept and which are difficult? The key to understanding and accepting our whole selves may lie in understanding that for every positive quality we possess we may have the opposite quality to a degree. Integrating these polar opposites and releasing self-judgment helps us to accept our true selves, which can relieve the turmoil that causes some nightmares.

✳

KAREN'S RECURRING NIGHTMARE

I am ashamed to tell anyone this dream. It is very disturbing. I would never ever do anything like this in real life. I keep dreaming that I am

killing my husband. Last night, I stabbed him over and over. In past
dreams I have suffocated him or shot him. These dreams leave me really
shaken up and I keep thinking about them during the day. I feel guilty
even though I haven't really done anything. This is really driving me
crazy.

A religious and nonviolent woman, Karen was very upset by her
nightmares. When probing a bit into the state of the marriage,
however, she confided that things were not going very well. She felt
controlled by her husband. "He doesn't listen and doesn't seem to
care about my feelings. He is under a great deal of stress at work
and is angry all the time. I think he takes his frustrations out on me.
He is constantly putting me down." Being unable or unwilling to
discuss her feelings with her husband, she forced her unconscious
mind to express her stress through her dream state. Karen's dreams
made it clear that action needed to be taken to relieve her repressed
anger and keep bigger problems from developing in her marriage.

Karen got the courage to talk with her husband. He was not
aware of the impact his unkind words and angry behavior were
having on her. They bought a series of relationship-building videos
and watched them together. The tapes helped, and Karen and her
husband are planning a trip to Hawaii—a second honeymoon.

✶

INTRUDER DREAMS

Another common nightmare involves an intruder, a frightening figure who breaks into your home. Since your home is your shelter, it
is often symbolic of the body, which houses the soul and mind.
Therefore, the intruder may represent an aspect of the self that is
emerging from the unconscious (unknown) into the conscious. Intruding thoughts can be represented by this nightmare. If you experience this dream, ask yourself, "Who or what is intruding in my
life, destroying my feeling of safety or security?" Solving this mystery will allow you to correct the situation in your waking state,
and you should stop having the dream.

An intruder can also represent unwanted sexual attention. If this applies to you, make it very clear to the person that you are not interested. The goal is to feel in control of the situation. So, when an intruder shows up in your nightmare, ask yourself "What new or unfamiliar feelings or thoughts have been breaking into my peace of mind?" Pay special attention to those you try to dismiss or ignore. Next, do your best to explore the thoughts or feelings and take the necessary action to empower yourself.

Intruder nightmares may also appear as a result of rage and anger. Everyone gets angry, and it is a natural and appropriate response when someone takes advantage of us or takes something from us. The best way to avoid being troubled by anger is to learn to express it constructively. Try to express anger at the time you first experience it. For example, if your friend is a half-hour late for a lunch date *again* without so much as a phone call, you may feel taken advantage of. Your time is just as valuable to you as theirs is to them, so say so!

Often we are so concerned about not hurting someone's feelings that we do ourselves a disservice and carry around anger or resentment until it haunts our dreams with unsettling images or explodes in ways we later regret. The remedy is to make your feelings known. If you are experiencing miscommunication or an unhealthy lack of connection, your dreams may also include symbols such as telephones, phone booths, letters, walkie-talkies, or other modes of communicating. Or your dream may have you in a place with others who are ignoring you or are unable to hear you.

The remedy, whenever possible, is to talk it out. In the late-for-lunch scenario, the interaction might sound like this: "I feel that you are not considering my time important; you are continually late when we have plans. This makes me feel angry and sad. I believe that you don't value our friendship." Then, give the other person time to respond. Most people don't mean to be inconsiderate. Since no one has the courage to confront them, they don't realize the impact their lateness (or whatever inconsiderate thing they do) is having. They will probably apologize, say they didn't realize it had happened more that once, and maybe offer to buy lunch. You will have done them a favor by helping them to recognize a behavior that is self-defeating, and you have just strengthened your friendship by caring enough to be honest. Most important, you empower yourself by communicating honestly in the moment and, you won't have to re-experience disturbing dream images, which reflect your held-in resentment or need for communication.

JAYNE'S PIRATE NIGHTMARE

I am stranded on a deserted island with other women. We see a ship and get excited and hopeful but, after they rescue us, we realize they are pirates. They throw us in a hole and we overhear their plans for us. We organize our escape and begin to fight them. There is blood everywhere. We kill them, but they get up and chase us again. No matter what we do we can't permanently kill them.

Jayne's nightmare depicts a helpless feeling and a loss of personal power. She needs to ask herself, "Who in my life seems to rescue me and then tries to hold me down? Who am I angry with for misrepresenting themself? Who seems to keep hurting me even after I think the worst is over?" The other women represent other parts of Jayne. Since blood represents the life force, we can guess that a lot of energy is being spent on this conflict. Pirates take what they want without regard for the needs of others. Jayne should evaluate her life honestly and ask if anyone is behaving in that manner.

Since the nightmare recurs, Jayne needs to take a good honest look at her life. She may not realize it, but her dream describes feelings of being stranded; rescued; temporarily hopeful, but then harmed; threatened; and hopeless. It takes courage, but everyone is entitled to live the life they want to. Finding that life may also involve sacrifice. However, being pursued without end and feeling you can never win is certainly not a good life. Discovering where in her life this applies is the foundation for change.

✳

Disaster Dreams

A dream of a plane crash, earthquake, flood, fire, or other disaster is another nightmare theme. Often, people are so disturbed by these images that they wonder if they are precognitive. Most often, these dreams reflect a major change in the life of the dreamer. There are, however, reports of dreams that did come true (see Chapter 9 on precognitive dreams for more on this phenomenon). Usually, though, these dreams reflect emotional upheaval. A move, divorce, change of career, financial problems, a baby's birth or any major change can be depicted as a disaster because of the dramatic way your life is affected.

IF YOU EXPERIENCE frequent nightmares, to the point that you dread sleeping for fear you will once again be terrified, or you don't want to remember your dreams because they are unsettling, you can take steps to eliminate them. Whether the source of your nightmare is stimulation from a heavy late-night meal, a terrifying movie, a fear or phobia, an uncomfortable circumstance you are involved in, or a distasteful personal characteristic, the first step toward eliminating a recurring nightmare is to understand what is causing it. After writing down your dream and processing it (according to the steps in Chapter 4), pay close attention to your feelings about the dream and the action in the dream. Then, ask yourself where in your life you experience similar feelings in the waking state. As to the action in the dream, ask yourself where a similar action or the metaphor for the action occurs in your life. If, in your nightmare, someone breaks into your home and you have to hide in a closet, ask yourself where in your life you feel intruded on? What uninvited person is in your space? Who frightens you? What circumstance in your life makes you want to hide? What or who makes you feel that you need protection? Continue asking every question that comes to mind until you feel that you understand the source of the dream. Once you have identified the origin of the fear, take steps to change the situation. If this feels too overwhelming, seek professional assistance or enlist the aid of friends or family. Understanding the source of the frightening images in your dream will nearly always release you from the nightmare. Our nightmares serve to prepare us for change, warn us of inner conflict and make us aware of the stresses we need to resolve. In truth, they are excellent guides in our quest for self-understanding.

Healing Dreams

About the second century B.C. at the Temple of Aesculapius in Greece, one of the first known instances of dreams being used in healing rituals took place. After purification rites and sometimes sacrifices or offerings, the person seeking healing was told to sleep and incubate dreams. The hope of the sick person was that Aesculapius, the Greek god of healing, would either miraculously heal their ailment or that he would come to them in their dream with a prescription for their cure. At the very least, they expected him to send them a dream that would offer a healing suggestion.

If the individual were too ill to make the trip himself, a servant or friend would stand in for him. And that associate's dream would be interpreted as the healing message for the person suffering from the incapacitating illness. Many people today report dreaming of others and feeling compelled to phone them the next morning to check on their safety. In some cases, the person dreamed of is simply symbolic to the dreamer and represents some aspect of the dreamer him or herself but, in other documented cases, a health warning is relayed through a loved one who is in a position to assist the subject of the dream.

If the person were not cured during the night, in ancient times he or she would share their dream in the morning with the other patients and the healers of the temple. They would discuss the prescription for the incubant and then act accordingly. Some did experience a cure, others were relieved of their symptoms at least temporarily and some were not helped. The interesting thing is that the dream was the vehicle of the cure.

Today, many people report having dreams that they feel are responsible for healing them or preventing accidents. Sometimes, the dreams offer a literal suggestion of certain foods or supplements. In other cases, the dreams offer warnings, such as to avoid a particular route often taken to work.

If you have a dream in which a doctor or nurse appears, you are probably being given health information to consider. (Unless of course, you *are* a doctor or a nurse or you work in a hospital, in which case the dream may have an altogether different meaning.)

Often, dreams are more symbolic than literal. Look for images such as a house or a vehicle, both of which can represent your body. The house symbol makes sense, since your mind and spirit are housed in your body. The front door may metaphorically represent your heart, the stairs your spine, the kitchen food and digestive matters, the bathroom cleansing and releasing of what you no longer need, the basement your subconscious mind, and the attic your spirit or higher self.

In the vehicle example, look first to the particular type. Is it modern or old-fashioned, fast or slow? What condition is it in? A bicycle requires balance and in a dream could indicate that you do also—or it could be a literal suggestion to get more exercise. An old clunker car that has a hard time making it up a hill can be telling you that it is time for a tune-up yourself. Healing dreams require careful interpretation. If you believe that your dream is telling you something about your health, talk your suspicions over with your physician.

MARY'S DREAMS

I dreamed I was a beekeeper and was eating honey all day long. I was very thin, even though I seemed to be consuming an enormous amount of sweets. Then, I dreamed that I was a man out on the prairie at least a hundred years ago. I was starving to death. I felt my stomach distended and a profound sense of hunger and despair.

Soon after having these dreams Mary was diagnosed with insulin-dependent diabetes, a disease involving the body's inability to process sugar, and one that can result in severe weight loss. In retrospect, her dreams seem to have forewarned her about a serious medical condition.

RON HAD A DREAM IN WHICH HE TALKED WITH GOD

Ron was in the hospital, very ill with pancreatitis. While in intensive care he experienced what he described as a thirty-six-hour dream.

In my dream I had a conversation with God. I said, "God—if it is my time, I'm ready to come home to heaven. And, if you aren't finished with me here yet, I'll stay. But let's get on with it because I can't take this extreme pain."

When Ron awoke, it had been a day and a half since he had last been conscious. He said he knew then he would recover and, from that moment, the pain lessened. After he requested that the doctors remove his morphine drip, his healing progressed rapidly. The doctors told him that quick recovery in a case as complicated as his was exceptional.

⁕

DON CLAIMS HIS DREAM SAVED HIS LIFE

Don says that his life was saved by a dream. For twenty-three years, Don lived with an addiction to heroin. At his low point, he said he was among the walking dead. One day, he found a spark of desire and courage to live and he admitted himself to a hospital.

During his first few days there, Don realized how very sick he was. He began praying for help to a higher power. On the fourth day in the hospital, he experienced the following dream:

I found myself floating weightless under water. I was able to breathe in this blue-black water. It was nighttime, and the water was charged with a powerful light of its own. I could see clearly for a great distance under water. I could also see the land above me, a huge city lit up in the night sky.

Swimming all around me was a small school of large, silver fish that I knew were salmon. They gathered around me in a protective circle. Then, one at a time, each of them broke from the circle, came to me, and swam into my heart, head, and body. They wiggled and shook their way through me and then out of the other side. One stayed in my heart. From there he leaped, swam, and shimmered light all through me. I felt an incredible, caring love and power in my poor, sick shell of a body. When I woke from this dream I knew that my prayer for help had been answered.

Don did recover, though not without a lot of hard work. He spent many years in twelve-step programs. Because of his dream and subsequent healing, Don was lead to shamanism. In the Native American version of this religion and philosophy, animals are seen as powerful guides to spiritual growth. The salmon in Don's dream contributed to his healing, but salmon are also known for swimming upstream. In his own way, Don also had to go against the current to get his life back on track. The journey was a very challenging one but, encouraged by the imagery of his dream and the support of others, he made it. Don was able to learn and grow from his experience; he decided to become a healer and help others.

Now he uses dreams in his healing work. According to shamanic principles, average dreams are not of much interest but big dreams are. These dreams are distinctive, in that they either serve to warn you for your protection or advise you of an upcoming blessing. Dreams are also used to make the soul receptive to an upcoming healing session. The patient is encouraged to ask his or her dream state to prepare the soul for healing in advance of the session with the healer.

Don's story is an example of how a dream not only helped someone change his life, but also actually helped him save his own life!

EILEEN'S HEALTH-WARNING DREAM

For years I've had a recurring dream that I am choking. I wake up, sit up in bed, and try to cough up whatever is caught in my throat. Sometimes, I dream it is a barrette, a hairpin, or gum. I upset myself and my husband. What does it mean, and can it be stopped?

This is a dream that must first be taken to a physician. It is possible that during sleep the air passage is actually closing, and the choking sensation wakes the dreamer so that she can change position and breathe. The physician may want to run some tests or observe the dreamer's sleep in a monitored sleep clinic.

Our minds will take the stimuli around us and incorporate them into our dreams. I once had a dream about sitting around a campfire singing, only to be woken by my father telling me to run outside because the cabin we were staying in was on fire!

THE INTERNAL HUMAN chemistry affects the entire psychic life, and an illness may be felt subconsciously before the actual physical symptoms present themselves. In some cases it is the disturbance to the psyche that is the cause of the budding illness. This could explain why dream diagnosis was emphasized in the clinics of Aesculapius. Unlocking your own power to tune into and consciously recognize the state of your health is possible through careful attention to your dreams. Your unconscious mind may know the status of every cell in your body and it may be easier to tap into this innate intuition in the sleep state because the self-will is subordinated. Sometimes, we must get out of our own way, putting aside any preconceived thoughts, which may be based on denial or wish fulfillment, to get in touch with the truth. We owe it to ourselves to take an active role in maintaining our health and well-being. Today's doctors have access to more knowledge and healing tools than ever before, but few consider themselves magicians or mind readers. You know your own body better than anyone else possibly can, and sharing the intuition gained from your dreams with your physician can result in the best health care possible.

CHAPTER
NINE

Precognitive Dreams
and ESP

People who have never had a precognitive dream may doubt that they exist, but many dreamers know that some dreams offer a glimpse of the future. While explaining these phenomena can be difficult, many believe that dreamers have access to the past, present, and future in the dream state.

Some of us dream of winning lottery numbers or the names of winning horses. Others dream of impending disaster. Many dream of someone they haven't seen in a long while and then actually run into them or hear from them within days. The following dream may have saved a life.

I was driving my car. My wife was beside me and my parents were in the back seat. As we went around a bend on a four-lane highway, another car, a white Chevy coming from the opposite direction, was going too fast. He couldn't stay in his lane and he swerved into mine, facing me head on. I woke sweating and anxious.

My mom was into dreams, so I called her that day and told her my dream. She said that it sounded like a warning dream. She asked if I could identify the road I was driving on. It was rural, but there were businesses along it. Still, I couldn't be sure of the exact location. Even though the dream was vivid, as I got on with my life and responsibilities I forgot all about it.

One weekend, my brother and his wife invited my wife and me to a barbecue, and he asked me to bring our parents along as well. My wife sat beside me, my parents in the back seat. As I approached a bend in the road, my dream came back to me. I glanced at my mother in the back seat and immediately changed lanes. She looked back knowingly as if she had the same thought I did. Just then, the exact car from my dream—a white Chevy—came around the curve going too fast. Had I been in the lane closest to the double line, the one I had just moved from, we would have been hit so hard I am sure we would have all been killed. I have five kids. I am so grateful for this dream and the warning it provided.

✳

JANE SEYMOUR'S DAYDREAM
SAVED A LIFE

Actress Jane Seymour had a precognitive daydream that saved the life of her small child. Showering while her nanny watched her two small children, suddenly she knew that the babies were in danger and she saw a vision of tragedy. She ran from the shower to her backyard, where she found one baby at the bottom of the spa and the other, who was just over three, not knowing what to do. The nanny had only gone in to answer the phone. Jane's swift action—taking her vision seriously—saved her child's life.

✳

TITANIC DREAMS CONTINUE

The first ship thought to be unsinkable, the *Titanic* hit an iceberg and went down on April 14, 1912. Afterward, many people came forward reporting that they had experienced dreams foretelling the disaster. One woman dreamed of her mother in a crowded lifeboat and could tell that the boat was about to capsize. The fascinating part of the story is that the dream occurred before the *Titanic* sank— indeed, the daughter knew nothing of her mother's passage on the ship, as she was surprising her daughter with this visit!

After the release of James Cameron's Oscar-winning movie *Titanic*, ninety-year-old Renée Mason remembered an old can of newsreel footage her husband had owned. Mr. Mason had worked for a news bureau and had been given the historic footage of the *Titanic* as a gift. He had since died and Mrs. Mason hadn't seen or even thought of the film for decades. She had no idea where it was. Before going to sleep, Mrs. Mason focused on the question, "Where is that news reel?" Upon awakening, she said, "the words 'in the shed under the bench' were in my head." Sure enough, when she went to look, the missing film was there, and was recently auctioned off at Christie's in New York for undisclosed thousands of dollars.

Certainly Mrs. Mason may have simply forgotten the location of the film. After all, the unconscious mind is a holding tank for everything we have seen and done in our lives, while our conscious mind can only focus completely on one thing at a time. Even so, it is wonderful to have a way to retrieve things long forgotten.

✳

PRECOGNITIVE DREAMS

While things we have forgotten, such as the location of a misplaced item, can sometimes be recalled through our dreams, what of dreams with no possible history or memory? Many scientists have set out to prove or disprove dreams as precognition.

In the 1940s, Viennese psychologist Dr. Wilfred Daim conducted a series of experiments. Numerous colored geometric shapes were put into sealed envelopes. One envelope was chosen, and a subject would take the random shape out of the envelope and focus on the image. He or she would then imagine "sending" it mentally to a sleeping subject. Sometimes the sender and receiver were miles apart. The exact time of the sending was noted as well as the time the dreamer woke and recorded his or her dream. Time after time, the image would work its way into the sleeper's dream. The results were published in the *Parapsychological Bulletin* of Duke University in 1949.

Dr. Montague Ullman, a psychiatrist and parapsycologist, conducted his own version of these tests in 1960 at the Maimonides Medical Center in New York. Using state-of-the-art machines to monitor mental activity during sleep, the sender would make a simple drawing and imagine "sending" it to the sleeping subject. In another version, after the experiment, the sender would concentrate on a piece of artwork chosen for its vivid and simple image and try to "send" it. In time, even more complex images were used. The upshot was that Dr. Ullman documented thousands of dreams that had significantly similar imagery to those that were "sent."

PAM SAW HER FUTURE

In the first dream, I am an angel floating in the corner of a family room I have never seen before. I am looking down at the back of my father sitting in his recliner; a woman I have never seen is standing to his left. They are gazing out into the backyard.

I originally had this dream when I was twelve. Some parts of this dream have come true over the years. I am wondering if the other parts may come true at a later date? Years after I first had this dream my parents divorced and the woman I saw in my dream became my stepmom. We lived in the house in my dream as a family. In a second dream, my stepmom, brothers, sisters, and I are standing behind an arcade building on a piece of property my dad owned. We were discussing what we should do with our dad's business now that he was dead. Our stepmom said we should sell. . . .

DREAM TELEPATHY

Some people report having the same dream on the same night as someone who is close to them. Identical twins Tia and Tamara

Mowry, best known for the TV show *Sister Sister,* often do. In one case they each dreamed of a tornado. Tornadoes can represent rapid thoughts spinning out of control, taking innocent victims along for the ride. Such chaotic thought could include worry, gossip, or negative thinking that is getting out of hand. In Tia and Tamara's case, it may reflect the spin of the media and tabloids, which are always looking for a story and are sometimes willing to stretch the truth or invent it. The Mowry sisters are devoutly religious and would want no part of scandal. Still, it must be a consideration for them and all who are in the public eye.

✳

FRANK AND RACHEL DREAM TOGETHER

A psychic sympathy often exists between people who share a bond of love or family ties. Frank felt that he and his girlfriend of two years were growing apart. They had been close during their last two years of college, but her studies were taking her to Israel and his job would keep him in New York. She was taking a vacation with her family before her move to Israel. He offered to pick her up from the airport but he believed that visit would be their last, at least for a long time. The night before her return he had this dream.

I was flying—it was great! Then I noticed I was over a desert that looked almost biblical. There were softly curving sand dunes. Then I noticed a tent, something you would see in an Arabian Nights *movie. I flew down to the tent and went inside. The sand was warm and it felt like baby powder on my feet. There in the tent was Rachel! We kissed. It was the deepest, most connecting kiss of my life. I could still feel her lips on mine when I woke up.*

When I went to the airport to pick up Rachel, she said, "I have to tell you about the most amazing dream I had." It was the exact same dream I had! We decided it was a sign, and that we wanted to try harder to make it work.

※

ESP

....

ESP in dreams has been documented by certain sources and does seem to occur. ESP, or extrasensory perception, refers to the acquisition of information without using our five human senses. Precognition is a form of ESP that reveals information about the future. While research is hard to document, studies show that as many as 12 to 15 percent of dreams may predict the future.

While the scientific means for proving ESP in dreams may not yet exist, anyone who has had a dream that came true has no doubt. Precognitive dreams can be hard to distinguish from normal dreams but these characteristics stand out:

- The dream is exceptionally vivid and intense.
- Sweating and trembling may occur.
- The dream often recurs.
- News broadcasts or written accounts immediately follow that relate to the dream.
- The dream leaves an impression that lasts for days or longer.
- For some dreamers, patterns occur, such as always having a certain dream before a major plane crash, or earthquake, even if the dream itself doesn't depict the disaster.

What should you do if you believe you've had a precognitive dream? Trust your instincts and your past experience. Take reasonable precautions when the dream includes a warning. Try to interpret the dream, to determine if there is a reasonable, symbolic meaning. Remember—actual ESP in dreams occurs in only a small number of cases.

Some people erroneously believe that they actually caused a

disaster because they dreamed it. This is absolutely false. Most dreams are symbolic and indicate what is going on deep within us. Disasters in dreams often refer to major emotional turmoil, or fear of it, rather than real disasters.

DREAMS
HAVE TWO
GATES

*Dreams surely are difficult, confusing and
not everything in them is brought to pass for
mankind. For fleeting dreams have two
gates: one is fashioned of horn and one of
ivory. Those which pass through the one of
sawn ivory are deceptive, bringing tidings
which come to naught, but those which issue
from the one of polished horn bring true
results when a mortal sees them.*

—HOMER,
The Odyssey

Dreams of Flying

Flying dreams are among the most fantastic and exciting that most people experience. Whether flying aided by your own arms, wings, a jet pack, hot-air balloon, or plane, flying dreams seem to fall into two categories. The positive and enjoyable variety can leave us, upon awakening, with the feeling that we have just returned from an adventure, and can offer an opportunity to rise above a situation for a new perspective. They can also provide a wonderful feeling of freedom from earthly concerns. Sometimes, they represent the desire of the dreamer to escape and avoid dealing with something difficult in the waking state.

The other variety can be more frightening, often involving plane crashes and a feeling of sinking or doom. If you are a passenger on a plane, you probably don't feel in control of the situation, just as when your future is in the hands of others when you are part of a team, group, or company. You may fear that the team captain or company management will make decisions that could be detrimental to you and that, through no fault of your own, your position could crash and burn. Planes can also represent higher status, a higher salary, or more prestige and, if the plane goes down, the fear of losing these things.

It is important to note that Sigmund Freud associated flying dreams with sexual desire—although he associated most dreams with repressed desires. Carl Jung, on the other hand, saw flying dreams as a desire to break free of restrictions.

Some dream of flying over their own neighborhoods, others fly into outer space. Every flying dream offers insight into your current situation. The following dreams may help you to better understand your own flying dreams. At the end of this chapter, questions appear that may provide you with additional insight.

A TRAVELER WONDERS IF
HIS DREAM IS PROPHETIC

I have had a recurring dream theme for the past seven or eight years. I either witness or am involved in a plane crash. I always walk away from the wreckage unhurt. However, the feelings I experience during the dream—of falling, being out of control, and fear of imminent death—are tremendous. I travel extensively for work and pleasure but, as a result of these dreams, my anxiety level increases prior to traveling. This is very draining emotionally and is becoming more pronounced as time goes on. I wonder if I will die in a plane crash.

The feeling of imminent death this dreamer describes is probably a fear of being fired as a result of circumstances over which he has very little control. In today's uncertain corporate climate, I would not be surprised if most executives, especially those in middle management, have this dream. Security can no longer be sought through company loyalty. We must all manage our own futures. My guess is that, seven or eight years ago, this man was promoted to a management position. While a positive step, it brings with it new stress, including the responsibility for others' productivity and the quality of their work. At the same time, a manager can't do others' work for them. He doesn't have the same control in a hands-on way and is forced to delegate and to trust. To a certain extent, his success is based on the quality of the work of others. This dream reveals the anxiety that goes along with this shift. The fear of losing status or financial security—a theme common among executives and others who have achieved a level of success in the corporate world, can cause anxiety, sleepless nights, and bad dreams. I suspect that the dream and the anxiety come more frequently prior to traveling and become more pronounced as the dreamer rises in status and title at work, since there is more to lose. Still, he always "walks away from the wreckage." So he should ride out the fear! The dream tells him that despite the fear he will always survive.

If you have similar dreams, these tips can help: 1. Save money and invest it. 2. Keep current in your field. Don't become obsolete. Read trade magazines; take weekend courses on the state of the art aspects of your industry. Make yourself indispensable. 3. Weed out any weak links within your employee structure, or get help for those who need it to improve and be more effective and efficient. 4. The last aspect, just as important as the others, is attitude. True security is knowing that no matter what life hands you, you will be able to adapt and move on. Reinforcing a sense of security should stop the dream.

MARION HAS BOTH TYPES OF FLYING DREAMS

A man is chasing me. I run fast, taking giant leaps, then I flap my arms and fly away, soaring in circles in the sky. People below look up in awe. I lose gravity and land safely, only to be chased again. In another similar dream, I am free flying, soaring happily above beautiful trees. I am wearing a nightgown. When I wake from these dreams, I am happy and refreshed. When I wake from the first, I feel tired and gloomy.

These dreams represent both good and bad flying dreams. The first shows Marion escaping from an assertive and dangerous life circumstance by flying—but she can't get away forever. Giant leaps can represent leaps of faith or a desire to run away from an issue. Remaining in a circular pattern means she doesn't actually get away, since going around in circles brings her back to where she began. Each time she returns to earth (her real-life circumstances), she must deal with the aggression again. Like Scarlett O'Hara in *Gone With the Wind* saying she will think about her troubles tomorrow, it buys some time but doesn't eliminate the problem.

The man chasing her could represent the male aspects of her personality, possibly her own aggressive nature that she is trying to avoid. Or, since males in the language of dreams are associated with being providers, the man may depict a bill collector! She is able to float her bills for a while. Her friends wonder how she gets by. Sooner or later, those bills come after her again and she is forced to deal with them.

In the second version, Marion is rising above her life's circumstances for perspective. She gains insight and feels relaxed, as evidenced by her nightgown. None of us can avoid life's problems entirely. She should try to determine what aggressive issues plague her, and take steps to deal with them, so that she doesn't need to escape. The second dream is one to cultivate and enjoy, like a little vacation.

A GRANDMOTHER FINDS PEACE

In my dreams I am able to fly by holding my arms in exactly the right position. I fly around just over the treetops. I see grass, flowers, fences, yards, rooftops, pets in yards, but not people. It is very liberating and extremely pleasant, not at all frightening. I hate to wake up! It is wonderfully freeing and exhilarating, I wish it would continue—or be real!

Dreams of flying can be either positive or negative. This one is definitely a good one. The feeling of freedom is actually the meaning of the dream. Rising above earthly concerns is an exhilarating experience. Since she doesn't see other people, she don't feel higher or better than others. Lighter than air, she is simply releasing herself from the heaviness in her life. These minivacations are part of our body's inner stress-management protocol. It is interesting, however, that this dreamer must hold her arms in exactly the right position to fly. Arms allow us to embrace and hold our desires. Others fly in numerous ways in their dreams. Therefore, this dream may indicate that if she is not allowed to function in the way she believes correct, her power will be limited.

Many dreamers express the desire for the wonderful dream they are experiencing to continue. They don't want to wake up, because the dream world seems better than their current life circumstances. Escaping into our fantastic dreams can be freeing. Our dreams can set the record straight, making us king or queen for a night! They can balance the stress of the day. While it is important to get out of bed and live our lives, it can be comforting, especially during times of stress, to know that we will again visit dreamland at the end of the day.

FLYING IN SLOW MOTION

I have been having variations of this dream all my life. I find myself in a dangerous situation and try to escape by flying, but can only fly in slow motion—just barely fast enough to stay aloft. Sometimes, my mother or my husband is in the dream and, when they are, I usually have to save them, too. When I wake up, I am often exhausted. My fear is that if I ever actually do find myself in a dangerous situation I will be powerless.

This dreamer can't get away from her thoughts. She tries to escape by flying, but is limited in how fast she can fly. When two close people in her life show up she has to save them, too. There is probably no correlation between her dream and her potential ability to cope with a dangerous situation in her waking state. Rather, the dream may indicate that when things get tough she desires to escape instead of dealing with the circumstances. Not that anyone would blame her! We would probably all rather escape than stay and work through something we feel is emotionally dangerous or unpleasant. Since her dreams sometimes include her mother and husband, it would seem that the danger could come from emotional entangle-ments with the very close people in her life. Since she has to save them, she may keep her own feelings to herself to avoid hurting them, but she also must save herself, and that requires making her needs known. Since air in the language of dreams represents thoughts and mental activity and, since she flies in slow motion, I wonder if she tries to push unpleasant thoughts out of her mind, rather than thinking them through and resolving them.

It can actually take more effort to avoid a situation than to just handle it. Since this is a lifelong recurring dream, she might try an experiment. The next time something comes up and she starts to bury it or change the subject, she should try to stay in the moment and resolve whatever it is. If she is with receptive people, I suspect she will feel empowered, and that the dream will change or stop al-together. If the dream persists after she attempts these suggestions, then perhaps assertiveness training or a communication class would be helpful.

A s k   Y o u r s e l f

When you have flying dreams, you may want to ask yourself these questions.

- By what means did I fly?
- What was the purpose of my flight?
- Was I in control during in my flight?
- Did I enjoy the flying in my dream?
- What does flying mean to me?

Dreams of Celebrities

Today, film and television stars have replaced the heroes and heroines of the past. Mythical figures are now often seen in a modern context. Mel Gibson or Denzel Washington may be seen in a dream representing the strong male archetype, and Sharon Stone or Julia Roberts might embody the image of feminine beauty. When you dream of celebrities, ask yourself what the person represents to you. The roles they have played may influence your description and your associations with them as dream symbols. Try describing the individual in five or six adjectives. What you think of them will determine their meaning in your dreams.

ROBERT REDFORD

I have always enjoyed Robert Redford's films, especially The Natural. *I think he is a good actor and director . . . good looking . . . but I have no special mania about him. He has been in a couple of my dreams.*

I dreamed I was in the Caribbean walking along the seashore. I see a very fancy cruise ship decorated with streamers and banners. At the gangplank, under a red awning, is Robert Redford, smiling and handsome in a white tuxedo.

Redford is the host and captain of the ship and he is welcoming everyone to come aboard. There is no fee, but you must leave all personal possessions behind. Everyone is gaily boarding and the seaside is strewn with luggage that will be left behind. I am drawn to him and the ship but am worried about going.

Soon, everyone has boarded, and the town is deserted. He asks what I am waiting for and I say I want to know more about this before boarding. He says he just wants to help people. Once aboard, they will never have any more troubles or sorrows and would never be hurt or hurt others. Everything will be taken care of for them. Of course, they will never make land again, never know true love, never know joy, and never be able to create or accomplish anything. Suddenly, I understand that he is Satan and that this ship is hell and I must warn those aboard. With this understanding, he no longer looks quite like Robert Redford, his suit turns black, and he laughs while I run from room to room trying to get people off the ship, to tell them the truth of their situation, but no one will listen.

We all desire escape from time to time—that is what real vacations are for, but this dream suggests the cost of bailing out and abandoning our unresolved problems (baggage) can be a loss of the good parts of life as well. Certainly, Robert Redford seems an attractive inducement to release the troubles of the day. While initially tempted, this dreamer has concerns. In this dream a ship would take her into the unknown, out onto the water, which represents the unconscious mind. However, she is not a blind sheep and is not willing to simply follow the others—she wants more information. The handsome captain tells her that if she chooses this voyage, she will never have trouble or sorrows. She should ask herself if she is currently troubled or concerned about being hurt or hurting others? Is she feeling like surrendering to someone or something to relieve herself from daily cares? This could be the dream of someone considering suicide or giving up in a battle with depression. It could also apply to someone considering using illegal drugs for escape or emotional pain relief.

To get the information she seeks, she has to give up her earthly possessions, and she will never make land again. Land represents what we know consciously. What a price to pay, never to feel joy again, or know love, or create anything! This sounds like death and, indeed, it turns out to be.

Now the handsome Robert Redford turns into a dark-suited Satan and the truth is revealed. This choice is hell! The dreamer tries to warn others not to make this mistake, but they won't listen. Here we have to ask who in her current situation is not listening to her when she knows what is best? Does she feel that she cannot persuade others? Are there people around her making bad choices? In her dream, she recognizes the cost of relief is too great and she makes the right choice.

For this dreamer it would seem that temptation and the desire to escape can look as good as Robert Redford, but only initially. Once the dreamer looks past first appearances she sees the truth and does the right thing.

*

MARRIED TO SALMA HAYEK

My wife is often told (and actually does) that she looks a lot like the beautiful actress Salma Hayek. I love my wife and, since there is a strong resemblance, I don't mind telling you that I find Salma quite stunning and beautiful.

My dream begins in a beachlike setting in Mexico, and involves Salma Hayek. We are enjoying a comfortable dinner at a restaurant on the coast.

My wife walks up calmly and joins us for dinner. We all have a pleasant conversation and I'm intrigued by what Salma is saying about how she lives as a beautiful and famous actress. When it is time to leave, my wife is no longer there, and I walk Salma to her gold convertible, where we share a quick, passionate kiss before we ride off together.

This lucky dreamer already has his dream come true! He is married to a woman he finds as sexy and sultry as the lovely movie star Salma Hayek. In this dream, Salma does represent his wife, at least in attractiveness and sex appeal. When both his wife and Salma are present in the dream, it is for conversation and nourishment. When he ends the evening, it is just Salma—again representing his wife. It would seem that he sees his wife as a star worthy of all that stardom has to offer—including a gold convertible!

ANTHONY HOPKINS
BECOMES A FAN

In the last six months, I have been part of a local community-college program for fine arts. My talent is singing. I have had two dreams, both of which were similar and had Anthony Hopkins in them.

In these dreams, I go to New York City to help recruit producers for an opera in which I have already been chosen to perform. At the dinners and parties, where the producers are wined and dined, I am asked to sing one or two of the arias from the opera, much like coming attractions at a movie.

In both dreams, Anthony Hopkins is present. He is a friend of one of the producers and he approaches me first by note, complimenting me on my performance. It is only at the end of the evening that Anthony Hopkins comes forward, introduces himself, and we share small talk. The attraction between us is strong and almost overwhelming. He asked me out for dinner and I am confused as how to respond, because I am married. I woke myself up at that point. I find Anthony Hopkins the kind of quietly intense man that I enjoy discovering. Both times I woke up regretting not going to dinner with him.

Anthony Hopkins is at the top of his career. He is as successful as an actor can be. His interest in this dreamer's work, especially in such a respectful manner, represents her own belief that her work is top-notch. She has confidence that she is worthy of recognition from the highest creative talent.

It would also seem that she has no desire to disrupt her marriage for her career, even though it is tempting. The temptation is actually a desire to merge with that star quality and feel equal to it. If she does have doubts about her relationship, she could try to play detective and discover the quietly intense qualities in her husband.

BRAD PITT PANTS

I had a celebrity dream that still makes me laugh. I am a forty-seven-year-old housewife, and Brad Pitt wanted me badly. In my dream I had to tell him that he was too young for me. I am not too old for him; he is too young for me. Important distinction!

Brad Pitt is fodder for fantasy! I think he is adorable!

Excellent! Forty-seven or not, this dreamer still feels desirable and attractive to a man considered to be one of the sexiest male actors of our time. This is a dream of great sexual confidence. You go, girl! This dreamer doesn't feel that age is a deterrent. Youth may be, but not maturity!

MY OWN DREAM OF BILL COSBY

When I first became a television host, I had a dream in which Bill Cosby invited me to tea. We were on a beach and then in his home. I was honored and excited even in my dream, realizing that he was an important television and movie star. He was so kind to me in my dream that I took it as a vote of confidence that I had found the right career. I saw him as a father figure because of his television program in which he played Dr. Huxtable. His character always gave such wonderful advice, and was a wise and charming father with a great sense of humor. I knew he was also involved with education and animated programs for children.

The beach is an area on the dividing line between what we consciously know and are aware of, represented by the land, and the unconscious or that which we are not consciously aware of, represented by water. I was looking for confirmation of my conscious desire to be an educator and to have a voice in the media. My dream of

Bill Cosby encouraged me to stick with my goals and make my dreams come true.

ASK YOURSELF

If you dream of celebrities ask yourself these questions.

- What is the star known for?
- How do I feel about the star?
- How would I describe the star to someone who had never heard of him or her?
- What would it mean to me to actually encounter the star?
- Who in my life reminds me of the star?

CHAPTER TWELVE

Dreams of Political Leaders

P*residents and royalty visit many sleeping people in* their dreams. These important leaders, past or present, are symbolic of the ultimate in power and authority. You may dream of consulting with these figures, going to the top for answers. If a leader befriends you in your dream, this indicates that you feel capable or worthy of higher rank in society. Read on to see how dreams of political leaders can influence your life and dreams.

THE PRESIDENT MAKES AN ANNOUNCEMENT

I can't figure this dream out and can't put it out of my mind. It starts with me going out onto a balcony. On other balconies are many people, all looking to the west. I am dressed in a nightshirt and look down at my legs, which look very strong. Then, the president comes out to the balcony and announces that the bombers and missiles are on their way to destroy the United States. I am really surprised and ask why. I am told that the rest of the world had united and become very aggressive. Their intent is to destroy the United States since it is the last bastion of democracy.

Balconies offer a higher perspective, a place to look out at the view. Others are there as well, so this dreamer doesn't feel alone in his perspective. The west seems to represent the United States and democracy. Dressed in a nightshirt, he has been caught in a resting mode. There may be a fear of sleeping through this dangerous situation. But his legs are strong—he can get away or take a strong stand in this matter. The president, the ultimate authority, makes a disturbing announcement. Perhaps this dreamer feels a deep concern for current military involvement and the policies of the west. Alternatively, this dream may represent a more personal situation, in which the dreamer is concerned about being victimized because of the actions of others in positions of authority. He may also have personal concerns about the authority figures within his circle.

THE DREAMER BECOMES PRESIDENT

I have just been elected President of the United States. The inaugural celebration is held in a swamp with hundreds of people celebrating my new status. As soon as I'm sworn in, two gray snakes come into the swamp. I take it upon myself as my first act as President to kill these two snakes with an ax. I kill the snakes by slicing them repeatedly. I am cheered on by the crowd. This was so vivid, but what could it mean?

President, swamp, and snake are the important symbols in this dream. It seems to indicate that the dreamer has recently taken on a new responsibility and feels swamped with work and new duties. Further, she has been given an opportunity to prove her leadership abilities. The new responsibilities make her feel bogged down by murky and unclear emotions. In the dream, she was elected, which suggests that she may not have volunteered for this position. Still, she rises to the expectations of the job and enjoys the attention of others.

Snakes have many symbolic meanings, although here they

seem neutral (gray), but they give the dreamer an opportunity to assert her authority. She is concerned about the snakes or deserters and decides to eliminate them before they can harm her or undermine her authority. Since she kills them by repeatedly slicing them with an ax, she may have some resentment and anger connected with her new obligations. She isn't sure how she feels about all of this or how it will turn out. Snakes are associated with deceit, and she wonders how long public support will last.

This could be the dream of someone just elected PTA president, or a corporate leader. She likes the new attention and may already be worried about how she will feel without it in the future when she is no longer in charge.

✳

PRESIDENT CLINTON IS VERY BUSY IN DREAMS

I'm an eighteen-year-old high-school senior. During the Monica Lewinsky scandal, I had repeated dreams about President Clinton. In one dream, I was asking him questions, one on one, and he was very nice. We were talking about life in general.

In others, though, I would be listening to him give a speech and he would be angry. I remember, in one dream, that during a press conference, he began electrocuting any member of the press who asked him about Miss Lewinsky.

And, in another, he was speaking in front of the White House and he began fighting with a Senate Republican. Clinton knocked the senator down and the president's shirt ripped along his spine in the process.

This dreamer is about to graduate from high school, she is newly adult, and she is obviously intelligent and aware of current events. She may wonder about the leadership of the world she is inheriting.

Much of the country was riveted as details became known in the Clinton–Lewinsky scandal. The nightly news became our soap opera. This dreamer put herself into the story. She feels personally involved in the events of the day and, it would seem, will make an informed and active citizen. In the first dream, "one on one," the president is amiable. Here the dreamer is shown that the authorities she will encounter will be respectful, even helpful to her. We could also imagine that President Clinton himself is a charming and polite conversationalist. So, the message is one of mutual respect—if she is respectful of authority that same respect will come back to her. Another spin is that the dreamer can converse with her own highest authority—her conscience. There is a part of each of us, some call it the overself, that knows the truth and knows what is in our best interest in any given situation. Many of us bypass tuning in or listening to this guidance, which is also referred to as *intuition* or *conscience.* We prefer to do it ourselves, and many times can get in our way or become our own worst enemy. This is much like a child ignoring the warning or advice of a loving parent. Meditation often leaves one with the feeling of aligning with these aspects of self, as does prayer. So, in this first dream, the president could represent this overself aspect for the dreamer.

Clinton becomes angry and defensive in the second dream, electrocuting those who bring up a subject about which he feels very guilty and would rather cover up. The common phrase, "if looks could kill," may apply here. His reaction to these prying questions probably did at times generate a dagger-eyed look. On a personal note, this dream may also be a warning to use tact and diplomacy even when the dreamer is right, especially when dealing with authority figures. I personally know of two people who lost their jobs for being right and waving it in the face of the wrong person. Dr. Joyce Brothers says it this way: "While most people don't like to admit it, diplomacy involves the ability to determine how much truth to present to others and how much to withhold in order to keep the peace." The dreamer may also be questioning her own ability to be authoritative when the situation calls for it.

The third Clinton dream is probably the most fascinating. Here, fighting with a member of the opposing party, the president's shirt rips open revealing his spine. In dreams the spine is associated with taking responsibility and with spinelessness, or lack of courage. So it would seem that this dreamer is trying to come to terms with the leadership of the country of which she is now a voting, tax-paying member. She may also have been disappointed by the authority figures in her personal life, seeing them exposed as spineless.

In *All Too Human: A Political Education,* George Stephanopoulos, former Clinton senior advisor, offers his personal account of his experience in the White House. The prologue of the book begins with a dream he had in January 1998, days after the Monica Lewinsky story broke and about a year after he left his position with the president. In the first part of the dream, Stephanopoulos is prepping the president for a network news interview. Word comes that a vague but terrible tragedy has occurred. The president responds eloquently and appropriately, making just the right statement, and Stephanopoulos is impressed and admires Clinton's ability even under pressure. Then, Stephanopoulos walks across the Oval Office into a very small, windowless room, which is bare except for nude pinups of Monica pasted on the walls.

Stephanopoulos writes, "I was struggling in my dream with the Clinton I loved and the Clinton I feared, the president I served and the man I didn't want to see."

It would seem that this young dreamer is also seeing both sides of authority and deciding for herself how she feels and what to believe.

DREAMS OF DICTATORS

I have had a series of dreams about Saddam Hussein, Hitler, and Milosevic. I am always a frightened refugee, deciding whether to do what the bloodthirsty, psychotic dictator wants me to do or to fight back and risk my life.

Oppression can begin subtly. Reading this dream, one has to ask, is there a dictator in the dreamer's life? A boss or spouse or parent who is at times unreasonable and exerts their will? Does she feel powerless in a situation? She may be empathetic to the innocents of the world, or she could feel oppressed herself. It could be time to take back the power in her life and free herself from a personal tyranny.

This could be the dream of an unhappy employee—or an abused wife. When faced with this type of dream, immediate action is indicated. Determine the source of the "dictator," and seek help from family, friends, doctors, or law enforcement as necessary.

THE QUEEN IS A RIOT!

Queen Elizabeth II is a scream of a joke teller in my recurring dream! Lavishly dressed women and men mingle and drink in an immense ballroom. Each guest is announced at the top of a formal staircase and grandly descends. Halfway down the landing, Elizabeth and I sit at a cabaret table. She is telling me hysterical bawdy jokes and wickedly dishing the arriving guests. We try to hide our giggles but then she reminds me that she is the queen and can laugh if she wants to. This only sends us further around the bend.

Finally Prince Charles appears. Elizabeth really lets loose on him. She makes a crack about his ears just as he approaches our table. Before I rudely laugh in his face I wake up. I always wake up laughing.

Waking up laughing sounds great—sign me up for that! The queen is known for her polished and reserved behavior. By seeing herself as equal to the queen, and when the queen's behavior is definitely out of character, I suspect this dreamer is justifying her own less-than-regal behavior and her love of gossip. She sits halfway down the stairway—a midpoint—indicating she is capable of both extremes, regal *and* bawdy behavior, though she feels a little embarrassed when lowering herself (down the stairs) and dishing others. The dream makes it acceptable to gossip, since the highest female role model is participating. After all, the queen even makes fun of her own son.

Perhaps the dreamer's upbringing didn't allow for such misbehavior. Her dream reassures her that it's permissible to bend the rules of etiquette and that judging others is natural—as long as she doesn't let it interfere with appropriate behavior.

ASK YOURSELF

If you dream of political leaders ask yourself these questions.

- Who are the authoritative or powerful people in my life?
- How am I affected by their presence in my life or by their behavior?
- What steps can I take to equalize the field?
- How can I maintain my own sense of power and control?
- Is there a political stand I want to take?

Dreams of Departed Loved Ones

It is quite natural to dream of a departed loved one during the grieving period. Dreams of those who have passed over to the spirit world can take two directions. In some, the person simply represents the characteristics you associate with them; hence, they become a symbol of whatever they represent to you—responsibility, humor, love, whatever you remember them most for. These dreams can occur at a later point in life in order to help you understand your current situation. You may also dream of the departed around the special dates you associate with them, such as their birthday, an anniversary, or the anniversary of their passing. This is the most common experience people have. Sometimes, though, in rare and often beautiful experiences, dreamers feel as though their departed loved ones have actually visited or communicated through the dream state. This seems especially common for those who did not get a chance to say good-bye to their loved one before his or her passing. These dreams offer consolation and reassurance.

In visitation dreams, many dreamers report physically feeling a presence—they may actually feel the touch of the loved one, smell the favorite cologne, or even cooking scents they connect with their loved one. Sometimes such a dream is accompanied by other phenomena, such as movement of objects, change in temperature in the room, or various light phenomena. While this may sound frightening, these very special dreams most often offer reassurance, closure, and support.

If you want to invite your departed loved one into your dream, have a personal item belonging to them near by, such as a photo; a letter from them; a cherished possession, such as an item of jewelry; or a letter to them expressing your feelings. Write your desire to dream of your loved one in your journal and decide that only positive, helpful, or loving images will be presented in your dream. As you drift off to sleep, think of your loved one, bringing them to mind with positive thoughts and memories.

Likewise, if you are having disturbing dreams of departed loved ones and you wish to put an end to them, I suggest the following. Put your request in writing in your dream journal or a note pad. Actively imagine your loved one moving on to a better place. Forgive them, if you can, for any misunderstandings or past actions; this will help release them from your unconscious mind. You may even want to write a letter of forgiveness in your journal.

Remember that forgiveness doesn't mean that the person deserves to be forgiven—rather, it means that you release *yourself* from being a victim. Whatever life hands us, no matter how unfair or wrong it is, it is up to us to learn, grow, and move on from the experience or stay stuck in the role of victim. As you drift off to sleep, ask to have a dream releasing your loved one to a better place. You may even want to visualize the person surrounded by light or angels.

Many people have a hard time forgiving. They believe that forgiveness implies that the actions of the other are condoned. Those who study these matters say that at the moment of death or shortly thereafter the individual remembers and re-experiences any pain they have caused from the perspective of the recipient. They may see right and wrong more clearly than they did on earth. We have no way to prove this, of course, but believing that there is balance and accountability in the afterlife can go a long way toward helping the living to let go and move on.

A GRIEVING WIDOW DREAMS OF HER LOST HUSBAND

My husband died two years ago after a lengthy illness. In my dream I said, "Arnold, come to me." My husband appeared before me, dressed in the white shirt, tie, and slacks he had been buried in. He had the most beautiful smile and his face glowed with happiness, health, and love. I said, "Arnold, touch me." As our hands touched, I felt an electric current run through my hand and up my arm. I know it is natural to dream of loved ones who have passed on, but the electricity generated by our hands touching baffles me.

We are electric beings. The brain and nervous system communicate through electric impulses. In fact, all matter is made of energy vibrating at its own precise frequency. Many believe that the spirit, which remains intact after the death of the physical body, is made of energy vibrating faster than any solid matter. This dream is a beautiful example of a positive after-death visitation. This woman requested contact with her late husband, and I believe the feeling of electricity she experienced is evidence that she did indeed connect with him. She should consider it a gift from him, proof that he still exists in a different form but is happy and remains loving toward her.

A MOTHER LONGS TO RECONNECT WITH HER DEAD SON

My oldest son passed away in 1985, at age fourteen. At least four times a year I have the following dream. I am sitting on the beach and I see him walking toward me. We are both overwhelmed with feelings of joy and contentment. I tell him how much I love him and have missed him. We hold each other for a long time and I actually feel him next to me. After a while, he says he has to go back. I have an instant fear of losing him all over again. I panic and beg him not to go. He says he has to, then smiles and disappears. I wake up with my heart racing and in a state of panic.

In the language of dreams, the beach represents the place where what we know (consciousness represented by the sand) and what we don't know (unconsciousness represented by the water) come together. It would seem, then, the perfect place for this dream to reunite her with her deceased son. As yet we have no scientific proof of an afterlife, but tell that to anyone who has had a near-death experience and they will just smile knowingly, much as the son does in this dream. In time, science and technology may be able to prove the existence of life after death. Since the dreamer describes the visits as joyful, I do not suggest that she make efforts to stop having them.

Still, losing the child again each time this mother dreams of him could be excruciating, unless she can change her attitude to one of gratitude for the additional time with him. We are not capable of understanding the "why" of these circumstances. We must be thankful that our children's lives continue in a new form and that we can meet them in our dreams. To avoid the panicky feeling that follows, the dreamer could remind herself that, even though he has to go back, he will visit again. He is obviously happy and does indeed care deeply for her.

*

A DAUGHTER WONDERS ABOUT WATER AS A DREAM SYMBOL

My mother has been dead since 1971. I dream about her fairly often. Almost every dream has some form of water connected to it, such as swimming pools, oceans, or tears. Does this have any meaning? I have been anxious about these dreams for many years.

Water in our dreams generally represents two things—the unconscious and/or the emotions. Swimming pools can represent contained emotion, the feelings we hold in. The ocean is a symbol of the unconscious, of emotion—and sometimes of the Creator, since one theory holds that humans evolved from the sea. Tears can represent emotional pain or joy but are associated with feelings.

This dreamer may have unfinished business—emotional uncertainty where her mother is concerned. As time goes on, there may be times when she misses her mother or appreciates her in new ways. Emotions she thought she had put to rest may resurface. If this occurs, she should write down her feelings toward her mother, expressing these ideas, whatever they are—anger, gratitude, love—on the pages of her private journal. This will make her more aware and may change the tone of her dreams. Writing her true feeling on paper can help her to understand and heal.

A LONELY WIDOWER
LONGS FOR TRUTH

My wife died seven months ago. For a year before she died, she could not walk and used a wheelchair to get around. Since her death, I have had this recurring dream at least twice a month. I arrive home and find my wife standing in the hallway. I say, "You've come back!" She answers, "Yes." She then runs to me and hugs and kisses me. She asks, do you want to know what happened to me when I died? That is when I wake up! It is great seeing her so happy and healthy, but I wonder what it means.

This dream is a beautiful evocation of the concept that the soul survives the death of the physical body. Many people report having similar "visitations" after the loss of a loved one. In *Talking to Heaven*, best-selling author and medium James Van Praagh writes that these are real opportunities to reconnect with our departed loved ones.

Seeing his wife happy and well-adjusted is a gift to help him with his grief. Since he continues to have this dream, he could try to stay in the dream long enough to hear her answer—what did she go through when she died? This gentleman's fear or grief could be waking him before he hears the rest of the story his wife offers to tell. Feeling comfortable with the truth will open the door to receiving the information his wife may actually want to share. He can facilitate this process by giving himself a suggestion before going to sleep, repeating, "Tonight I request a dream of my wife. I want to know what she experienced after her body died." By inviting this information he can clear the way to receive it.

MY GRANDMOTHER VISITS ME IN A DREAM

Several years ago my grandmother, whom I loved dearly, had passed over and I was devastated. I had been very close to her and her death came suddenly; I didn't get to see her before she died. One day, I was missing her particularly. I spent the day thinking of her and appreciating her presence in my life. I had her recipe box and I took the time that day to look at every recipe in the little box. I remembered times she had prepared many of the dishes. I traced her handwriting and smelled the paper hoping for a whiff of her familiar scent. That night when I went to sleep I was very troubled, so much did I wish that I could call her and ask her advice.

I went to sleep, and, then, at a certain point, I felt someone holding my hands. As I became more aware, I felt the hands in great detail. My grandmother spent her life sewing, gardening, and cooking. She had developed arthritis and her knuckles were enlarged and, at times, very painful. I felt her warm, soft, and gnarled hands. I could even feel the raised blood vessels she had. I wanted to open my eyes and see her. I was desperate to do this, but I had the feeling that if I did open my eyes, she would evaporate. Finally, after mentally sending her love and appreciation, I did open my eyes and, as I did, I felt the grip slowly release. No one could convince me that I didn't actually spend time with my grandmother that night.

A WOMAN DREAMS OF HER MOTHER
AND FEELS PAIN

Since my mother died at eighty-seven, I have had the same dream several times a week. She is still alive but has another health problem. I keep telling her that she is dead, but she has a new illness in every dream. I took care of her for the last several years of her life. It is disturbing to me that I have to relive her death in my dreams.

This dreamer may want another chance to do a better job at caring for her ailing mother. Often, if we feel we didn't do everything we could, if we feel guilty, we have to relive the experience of our loved one's passing. We will all die sometime. Often our caregivers may feel distraught. No matter how good a job they do, in the end our bodies will give out. Unlike other jobs, where performance produces a happy ending, in caring for a dying loved one the objective is to make them comfortable, but the ending can rarely be described as happy for those left behind. She needs to let go of her reenactments and move on. No amount of caregiving could have saved her mother's life.

She could try writing her mother a letter, telling her everything she needs to say and placing the letter beside her bed. This should release any feelings of guilt and also release her.

A WIFE MOURNS AND WONDERS

My husband died three years ago. Since then, I continually have this dream. There is a white house or apartment. The carpet, walls and everything inside are white. He is always in it. Sometimes he talks to me, but most often he tells me to go away. He says he doesn't want me anymore. We were married for thirty-nine years, so this is quite disturbing.

In his own way, this woman's husband may be telling her that he wants her to live. By saying he doesn't want her anymore, he may just be communicating that it is not her time. It is also possible that he simply represents the afterlife for which she is not ready. She should focus on the good times, the love they shared, and the happy moments. While alive, live!

This dreamer also feels rejected by her husband. He left her and death is the ultimate rejection. She may be angry. Yet how can one express anger toward a departed loved one? One way is to write down your thoughts; another is to talk with compassionate friends; if this is not enough, counseling maybe in order.

ASK YOURSELF

If you have dreams of loved ones who have left this plane and you want to understand the dreams better, try asking the following questions:

- Is my dream a positive experience?
- What feelings and emotions do I have as a result of the dream?
- How would I describe my loved one to someone who never met him or her?
- Is there anyone currently in my life that has the same characteristics, or reminds me of, this person? (Your loved one may be a symbol of someone else.)
- If I had to answer yes or no, would I say that I had actually experienced my loved one through my dream?

Dreams of Relationships

*O*ur relationships frequently play into our dreams, indeed it is common to dream of our family members, even those who have died. Dreams of fellow employees and those we encounter in the work environment are also common, as are dreams of romantic partners past and present. If you dream of a current partner, that individual may represent themselves, but they may represent everyone in their gender or even a part of you.

Some people dream of family members, and feel that the dream is a warning. Mother's intuition and other bonds of love can at times stimulate such dreams. If you feel you have had such a dream, refer to the chapter on precognitive dreams for further understanding.

The most important relationship in each of our lives is often also the most overlooked. That is our relationship with ourselves. The knowing and understanding of our bodies, minds, and spirits define this relationship. Within each of these parts are levels of awareness that we unpeel layer by layer as we mature and as we seek inner knowing. The conscious, or overself, is the captain of our ship, but sometimes it seems that we stop listening to its wise guidance as we seek to steer the boat ourselves. The result can be mutiny and confusion, or even a disastrous sinking of the ship.

For a time, award-winning actor Kelsey Grammer seemed to be sailing without benefit of his ship's captain. He made no secret of the fact that he struggled with many aspects of his life and that this struggle could be his undoing. Kelsey had suffered from many tragic losses in his family and had spent time in the Betty Ford Clinic for help in dealing with drug and alcohol abuse. His dream demonstrates the fascinating and very personal approach the subconscious mind can use to get us back on track in the relationship with ourselves.

*

KELSEY GRAMMER'S INNER MOTHER

This dream was so vivid it woke me up, but I have no idea what it means. I dreamed my mom was calling the play-by-play at a Miami Dolphins game. She was very professional and was doing a great job.

This is a powerful and life-changing dream. It means that Kelsey's emotional and nurturing aspects, represented by his mom, know the rules and are calling the shots in his game of life. Dolphins are sea creatures. Since the ocean is symbolic of the unconscious, and the air symbolic of conscious awareness, the dolphin—known for jumping from the water through the air—is a messenger from his unconscious mind. A part of Kelsey is always aware of what is going on and what is right. I suspect there is also a rebellious adolescent part of him that, at times, doesn't want listen to this voice of reason.

Dolphins are also often portrayed in the media as rescuers. Kelsey's dream reminds him that, when in doubt, he should imagine asking his "very professional" mom what to do and take her advice. Mom here represents authoritative guidance, the one who does know the right way to proceed. If he does this, he will be playing by the rules and his choices will turn out for the best.

Currently, Kelsey is at the top of his career and is also reported to be very happy with his lovely wife.

STILL DREAMING OF HER EX

I have been married for over twenty-five years but, at least twice a year I have a powerful sexual dream about my ex-boyfriend. I have four children and my marriage is okay, but this guy is still very much in my heart. Why is this feeling so strong?

It is not at all unusual to dream of a past love. Past lovers represent a freer, less encumbered relationship when the responsibilities of marriage and children didn't interfere with the spontaneity of romance. When we dream of old lovers, especially in a sexual way, our dreams are expressing our longing to connect with the qualities we associate with that person. Of course if you do have literal desires for this person, even awake, that's another thing but, most often, the past lover is symbolic of the good qualities and times that you remember—excitement, freedom, youth, and the like. Some women and men even experience orgasm during these dreams. Great bonus! Some people feel as if they have cheated on their mates, but they needn't feel guilty.

Once we become sexually active adults, we may dream of sex during periods of abstinence. Sex is a human need. Perhaps it's time for this dreamer to plan a romantic getaway with her husband and spice up the passion!

ONE WIFE'S DREAMS OF HER HUSBAND

I was traveling to Hawaii by plane with my husband. We were supposed to be taking off, but I felt as though we had been taxiing too long. Looking out the window, I realized that we were on a freeway! Suddenly, I found myself lying on the freeway with my husband. We weren't hurt, but the plane had apparently blown apart. Before we had time to get up, I saw a huge gasoline tanker truck jackknife. It was sliding directly at us. I looked at my husband and said to him very calmly, "We're going to die now." I wanted to be thinking the right things when I died so I turned to him and said, "I love you." At that moment, the truck stopped sliding and we were safe.

This dream shows that her marriage needs an injection of intimacy. Hawaii is considered a paradise: She seeks romantic bliss. It seems she's waited a little too long to take off and renew the romance in her marriage.

She survives the first disaster, a plane crash, but another is headed her way. A freeway represents an open path; this marriage could go anywhere from here. Saying "we're going to die now" refers to the marriage dying or ending, but expressing her love saves the day. This dream is a warning, a beautiful service provided by the unconscious. This dreamer should write her husband a love letter from her heart, sharing all the ways that she appreciates him, and renewing her loving feelings. Perhaps they can schedule a romantic getaway. Since they survived both near disasters, I believe they can save and improve their situation by sharing their love.

This marriage is on the tarmac and needs a lift. There is an unconscious fear that it will crash and burn (there may even have been two close calls already). Time for emergency measures. But all is not lost—there is love to be rekindled.

I WANT HIM OUT OF MY DREAMS

I was divorced five years ago, but I occasionally have a disturbing dream in which I am forced to live with my ex-husband, feigning happiness with him. Is there anything I can do in my conscious thoughts to rid myself of these dreams?

The unconscious mind is showing this dreamer that she is in a situation she doesn't want to be in. It feels forced and uncomfortable, like her marriage. She is keeping up appearances, pretending to be happy. She can ask herself where in her life this is occurring—in a new relationship, at work, with a friend? Discovering the source can help make a change. The former husband simply represents a relationship or obligation that makes her unhappy or uncomfortable.

*

MARGUERITE RECEIVED SPIRITUAL GUIDANCE

Marguerite was involved in an undefined romantic relationship. After dating Howie for about five months, he started an argument one evening over what seemed to be a very small matter. The relationship became strained. Marguerite believed that Howie was the one, the man she would one day marry, so she tried to be understanding and patient; she even felt that she must be responsible in some way. Howie at times seemed tender, at other times distant. He began calling less frequently. Many women in this situation would have moved on, writing this up to experience, happy she hadn't wasted more time. Marguerite, however, felt that he needed support—perhaps this was his way of testing her to see if she was wife material. She would prove to him that she cared by staying true to him and available to him. Meanwhile she became very stressed, lost weight, and even began a destructive pattern of pulling her own hair out one strand at a time.

During this time, Marguerite had the following dream:

I was at a party alone and I wanted to leave. As I was walking out, I saw a small kitten on a tree. As I got closer I saw that there was a thumbtack holding the kitten to the tree by one paw. I was startled. Was I the only one that could see this? I pulled out the thumbtack and the carcass fell to the ground. I assumed it was dead, but then the kitten came to life and ran away.

This dream was telling Marguerite that she was isolating herself from the party of life. The image of the crucifixion and resurrection comes to mind through the innocent kitten impaled to the tree through its paw. Thought to be dead, it comes to life again, once released from the restriction of the tack. Marguerite felt dead inside, but new life could be hers if she would just free herself from her self-imposed emotional imprisonment. Marguerite was not especially fond of cats in her waking state but, to her, the kitten was symbolic of her innocence in the situation with Howie; she felt that he had crucified her without reason.

However, it can take time to get over someone whom we feel we love, even when the love is not returned. Marguerite prayed for guidance and, especially, tried to communicate with the angels, asking them to show her the way to remove the pain from her heart. A few days later she had this dream:

I was at a party and had gone into the handicapped stall of a restroom. Two other girls were in there with me. A guy came in and was peering over the door. I was trying to shoo him away but the girls were just laughing, not helping at all. Next thing I knew I was being sprayed with a white, sticky goo. It was in my hair and all over. When I woke I realized it was semen, and I felt totally grossed out.

This dream again refers to life as a party and suggests that Marguerite should be getting back to happy times. She had handicapped herself by holding on to a bad relationship. In dreams, bathrooms symbolize physical and emotional cleansing, and toilet dreams deal with letting go of what no longer serves us. The oblivious, laughing girls may indicate that she doesn't feel supported by her friends or that she is not seeing the truth in the situation. The man could represent the balance of male energy. Instead of the weak, submissive female role, she needs to adopt a more masculine, self-sufficient attitude. He could also represent Howie, who certainly got more pleasure from the situation than she did. Through this dream, Marguerite came to the realization that she had been used for sex in her relationship with Howie. Marguerite believed that she had received spiritual guidance, and was finally able to let go of this relationship and get on with her life.

THE MOTHER-IN-LAW

My mother-in-law and I are at the airport together standing in front of the arrival and departure monitors. (My mother-in-law lives in Los Angeles,

I live in Chicago.) We suddenly realize what the date is and that, although we have to be back on a certain date, we have more time to travel than we thought and we get excited. We start thinking about where we should go. We decide to check out a ticket counter in a different terminal. There are no escalators. The only way to get from terminal to terminal and floor to floor is to use roller coasters that are in water, like a ride at Disneyland!

This relationship with the mother-in-law can go anywhere and the dreamer has more time than she thought to decide on a new way to define her relationship. A new destination or way of relating to her is ready to take off. However, there is no easy escalator to get them to the next level of their relationship. They have to go through the normal ups and downs. Part of the dreamer knows that it is safe and will work out all right, since she views the roller coaster much like an amusement park ride. The water part indicates that it is an emotional process. Since she mentioned departures, the word terminal, and having more time, I wonder if there was the threat of an illness for either of them. Or something else, such as a recent death in the family, that caused her to fear a shortening of their time together? Whatever has caused the emotional ups and downs, it appears as though this woman's bond with her mother-in-law is a valued and happy one.

A DREAM OF MOM

I have always had a very rocky relationship with my mother. Recently, after a huge falling-out with her, I decided for my own well-being to limit my exposure to her. I will have to be in contact from time to time regarding my siblings. Since the fight, I began having extremely vivid nightmares about her, ranging from just visiting her in Florida to her actually trying to kill me. The nightmares did stop for a few days, but now they are back in full force, often with three or four in one night. Obviously, they are affecting my sleep, as well as my emotional state.

These dreams about visiting your mother could reflect an inner desire to meet her half-way and reconcile, or a desire for a relationship that is simply not possible. This dreamer may wonder if for at least brief periods, when necessary, they could get along.

The dreams in which the mother is trying to kill her daughter are, of course, much more disturbing. Being killed in a dream is not too hard to figure out—we feel someone is angry enough to wish us out of his or her life. Even though the dreamer made a conscious choice to limit her exposure to her mother, to protect herself from volatile outbursts, it doesn't necessarily follow that every part of her has accepted this development. Since she is having so many nightmares each night, she is probably in emotional turmoil. There is an inner battle going on between three parts of self—there is the head, which knows intellectually what is in her best interest and has taken action; the heart, which feels wounded because of the lifelong difficulties with her mother; and the gut, which senses this is not how things should be and feels some sadness that the relationship is so bad.

I recommend two things. First, the dreamer may consider counseling to deal with the pain and disappointment. Second, she should find a good and supportive friend, a surrogate mother, so to speak, with whom she could share in a maternal way. Creating her own "family" can help fill out what is lacking by the estranged relationship. This support should ease the nightmares too.

In this particular case, it would seem that the dreamer made an appropriate choice. No matter how much we may yearn for a healthy relationship with family members, it requires that everyone is healthy to start with and that is not always the case.

A FATHER'S NIGHTMARE

My daughter is only thirteen and she isn't at all interested in dating or boys yet. So why did I have a terrible dream that she was riding on the back of a motorcycle with an older man who was going to teach her to French kiss?

It is not too surprising that the father of a teenage girl would have some anxiety about protecting her from danger and heartbreak.

The biker may embody his worst nightmare of a boyfriend. If he hasn't already, he should begin talking with his daughter about safety, self-respect, and when he feels it is okay to begin dating. Meanwhile, he could encourage group friendships and parties in the home so that he can meet and get to know her friends. By asking her about her day, keeping up with who her friends are, and not judging or teasing her, he could encourage open communication.

Parents can torment themselves with anxious dreams about their children. Fear for their safety can make them feel vulnerable and impotent. Raising them with good values along the way and keeping communication open can help relieve fear. And a prayer every time they leave the house couldn't hurt!

A s k Y o u r s e l f

When you have relationship dreams ask yourself the following questions.

- Is my relationship in need of first aid?
- What should I know about the current status of my relationship?
- What does the person in my dream represent to me, how would I describe him or her to someone else?
- Could the person in my dream represent a part of me? What part?
- Are certain changes in order?

CHAPTER
FIFTEEN

Dreams of Sex

In the language of dreams, sex is still sex! It is also other things, however. Besides the obvious—desire and passion—intercourse embodies the merging of qualities and characteristics of the principal parties. People dream of having sex with all types of partners, many of whom might seem inappropriate. While at times disturbing, the message of these dreams is often powerful and beautiful once understood, since sexual union indicates a combining of energies, a desire to be close to or take on the attributes of the other.

ONE SON'S DREAM OF HIS MOTHER

I consider myself a good son and I love my mother very much, but to dream about having sex with her? This has happened at least twice. I enjoy the dream very much. But when I wake up and remember the dream it is very disturbing to me. Is this considered normal, or what is really going on with me?

I understand the discomfort of this dreamer. At face value this dream reflects the ultimate taboo. Oedipus, according to Greek myth, unknowingly kills his father and marries his mother. From this story, Freud articulated the Oedipus complex, symbolizing a boy's early sexual attraction to his mother and jealousy of his father. Jung described an archetype called the Great Mother as a universal symbol. From the divine and virginal mother of heaven to the wicked witch of fairy tales, the Great Mother appears in our dreams to remind us of nurturing, fertility, maternal love, as well as possessive, dominating and seductive traits.

Since this dream is enjoyable and the dreamer only feels disturbed upon awakening, I see the dream as a positive one. The son is merging (sex) with the qualities of maternal love and creation. In the language of dreams, sex with a parent can truly be the desire to be more like the parent, more parental, or more grown up. Since feminine energy is associated with creativity, I would be interested to know if he is in a creative profession and feels inspired or more productive on the days after he has this dream. This dream offers me the opportunity to remind readers that no matter how disturbing a dream may be on the surface, once interpreted it is positive and helpful.

A VIRGIN'S DREAM

Recently, I have been having very sensual dreams about my boyfriend. In my dreams he is dressed like a biker. We have sex outdoors, late at night. I can feel every movement of his body and can hear the loud pounding of his heart as we make love. What is bothering me is that in real life I am twenty-one and still a virgin.

Since the woman is an adult and has a boyfriend whom she is attracted to, it would seem normal that she would imagine having a sexual union with him. We do have sexual dreams when we are not having sex—it seems to be a balancing mechanism. I interviewed one man the day he was released from prison and he said that his dreams were nearly all related to sex and family, the two things he didn't have access to while he was incarcerated.

She has this biker-guy image of her boyfriend in her dreams. I assume that this is not his normal appearance—maybe it is a fantasy image of the dangerous type of guy that some women find mysterious and sexy. Or, the biker may represent this dreamer's unconscious desire to break out of her virginal, good-girl image.

Dream sex is certainly safe sex! Dreams provide a truly safe place for sex and fantasy; they can be our private and secret place to explore. Of course, since she has waited this long, she should certainly wait until the time is right for her and, until then, just enjoy her fantasies in her dreams. In any case, her dream seems a fairly normal sexual release or balance dream and nothing to worry about.

POINT OF VIEW: BABY!

In my dream a man is having sex with a pregnant woman. I am in the womb. My sleep is disturbed by the rocking motion and I feel smothered. I awake from this dream in a panic, gasping for air.

If it is true, as some say, that it is possible to remember time spent in the womb, it would seem that this is one such memory. If, on the other hand, the dream is purely symbolic, then perhaps the dreamer is still developing in some way and feels creation rocking her boat! The feeling of being smothered and actually gasping for air could be a panic reaction based on a fear or concern for the success of this development or the pressure of a deadline. So, if we are to interpret this dream along these lines, she is developing something and feeling as though time could be running out.

Another woman had a dream of being in the womb in which she heard her parents arguing and she felt unwanted. Then she was gasping for breath and felt that her mother was smoking. It all felt very real. She was able to verify that her parents did have a specific and heated argument while her mother was pregnant and that her mother smoked at that time!

As bizarre as it may seem, this odd dream from the infant's perspective may actually be a memory. We certainly do dream of things we remember from early childhood. Hopefully, in the future, there will be more research available as to what a child *in utero* can actually perceive and remember. Many parents believe that their baby recognized their voices immediately at birth because of their efforts to talk, read, and sing directly to the infant during pregnancy.

If this first dream is an actual memory, we still have to wonder why it is showing up in her dreams now. Is something making her feel smothered? What comes to mind when she thinks of her dream? She will need to write in her journal and get in touch with deep feelings to understand this one. If the feelings of panic, anxiety, and/or difficult breathing continue, she may want to consult her doctor just to be on the safe side.

HOMOSEXUAL DREAM

I am a heterosexual woman. I appreciate women's beauty and have wonderful relationships with my girlfriends, but when it comes to sex, I definitely love men. I don't recall the entire dream but in one part I am having sex with a woman. I can't really see her face, but her body is athletic looking and could resemble women I have seen at the gym. This is a recurring theme. What does it mean?

It is not uncommon to dream of having sex with someone of the same gender. If you are homosexual, of course, the meaning may be more literal. But if you are not, it may leave you feeling uneasy. Some wonder, does the dream mean I secretly desire someone of my own gender? Am I gay?

Depending on the context and details of the rest of the dream, the dream may have many meanings. But a dream cannot make you gay—or straight. Whether you are homosexual or heterosexual, sex in dreams needs to be understood for the way it combines the energies and attributes of the people involved.

In dreams, men and women represent the qualities that we associate with each. Sexual intercourse combines these energies or qualities. Since the woman in this dream seems athletic, perhaps what the dreamer desires is a more athletic and healthy body. Perhaps she worries that this will make her seem more masculine and that prevents her from working out—but think again. Many feminine and beautiful women are sporting biceps these days.

SEX WITH A CO-WORKER

I am a happily married man. Why do I dream of having sex with the women I work with? I feel kind of guilty about this, but I truly have no desire to actually act on it.

I would wager that most working people have dreamed of sex with a co-worker at some time, even the happily married ones. Sex in a dream may not have anything to do with sexual desire at all. We reproduce quasifamilial relationships in the workplace. A woman's boss or colleague may be the surrogate husband. A male's co-worker or boss could be his surrogate wife, in the sense of sharing responsibilities, being accountable to one another, and so on.

When we dream of sex with a co-worker, we may be symbolically envisioning a merging of skills, talents, and abilities. We may see the right partner for a particular project or account by seeing the two of us hooked up in a dream.

One word of advice, though—it is probably best not to mention these dreams to either your spouse or the person you are dreaming about. Unless they really understand the dream-interpretation process, hurt feelings and misunderstandings could result. These are perfectly normal dreams and are no reflection of his feelings for his wife or marriage.

FUTURE SEX

My dream seems so bizarre it is embarrassing. In my dream, it is the future and very realistic robot-clones are produced as sexual partners. I am

in a showroom that contains both male and female robot-clones of all
races. A salesman takes my group through the showroom. He speaks of
how we can do anything we wish with the beings as they have no minds.
He begins to demonstrate by having sex with one right there in front of
everyone. He says that when you get tired of one you can trade it in or
discard it since it is not human.

In this dream the man can have any sexual experience he wants
without any complications. The robot-clones are simply objects, hy-
brid blow-up dolls. No conversation, no need to charm and win her
over, no love, no giggles!

On a purely sexual basis this might appeal to some. But why did
he have this dream and what does it mean to him? Does he objectify
women, seeing them only as sexual beings? Or, maybe the opposite,
he resents those who do treat or talk of others in this way? Women
have been objectified for centuries. It is my sincere hope that the future brings increased respect for all individuals. This dreamer could
be tired of the complications or high maintenance of his relationships, or he could feel that he is in danger of losing the personal
connection in his intimate relationships.

Perhaps there is a subconscious fear of the human factor being
removed from so many things—ATM machines have replaced the
bank teller, an automated voice answers our phone call at many
businesses, we buy stock online—that if things continue we will
one day take the human factor out of sex. This dream could then be
a message to nurture and reinforce personal relationships.

SEX WITH A CAMEL?

I was in bed having sex but, as we both climaxed, I opened my eyes and,
to my horror, my partner was a camel! I was so disgusted that I woke up
and felt nauseous.

Okay, before getting grossed out, let's take this dream apart and
look at the symbols. The camel can survive for days in the hot
desert without water, and so is associated with survival. A camel

also kneels to be loaded down with heavy merchandise or supplies and is therefore symbolic of humility, but it can also be mean-spirited and sometimes spit.

The meaning of this dream could be as simple as a desire to become a self-sufficient survivor or more humble in nature. The dreamer should ask herself if she could see her actual lover or herself as mean-spirited. Is this something she needs to pay attention to? When a dream is unpleasant, take a breath and break it down into separate components. It will make a lot more sense and set you at ease.

ASK YOURSELF

If you have sexual dreams ask yourself the following questions.

- Is my dream a purely physical release?
- Who is merging or combining in the dream?
- How would I describe the individual I am having sex with?
- Would I benefit by taking on their traits?
- What is my feeling about the dream?

Dreams of Pregnancy and Babies

In the mystical language of dreams, pregnancy can represent a creative project that you have conceived and are gestating or nurturing. This project could be a new business, a novel you plan to write, a painting, a song, a garden you want to plant. Of course, if you are trying to conceive an actual baby or are already pregnant, your dream could have a more literal meaning. Babies in dreams can represent giving birth to this new creative endeavor. They can also symbolize new beginnings, innocence, and untapped potential, and are considered to be good omens.

GYPSY WOMAN

When I was pregnant with my first child I had a dream that I was walking down a dark alley. There were sets of three stairs that led down to an open door. In the doorway stood a gypsy woman holding an infant. I walk

down the stairs toward the woman. She then handed me the baby, and it was a girl.

Then I turned to walk away with the baby in my arms and the dream ended. As it turned out, my child was a girl, but I had not known that prior to her birth. Then, two years later, I experienced the same dream while pregnant with my second child, only this time my two-year-old daughter was at my side. I met the gypsy woman again, and she handed me another baby girl. I again turned to walk away with the second baby in my arms. When my second child was born it also turned out to be a girl. Could it be that my body was trying to tell me the gender of each child? I find it interesting that I had essentially the same dream with each pregnancy.

Pregnant women often seem to have a bond through their dreams with their unborn children, and may be more psychic than others, at least where the well-being of their unborn children is concerned. This may be a natural protective form of communication, which falls under the heading of maternal instinct. The gypsy woman in these dreams is certainly an effective fortune-teller, since she did predict the future.

She may also represent the Great Mother archetype. This image can take many forms, and often appears in the dreams of pregnant women. The Great Mother in her positive sense symbolizes nurturing, fertility, and maternal love. The gypsy woman in this dream also brings to mind another archetype, that of the Wise Old Woman. She represents wisdom, knowledge, and strength of conviction, and may teach something of value in a dream. Dreams containing archetypes are often vivid, and can be recalled long after they were experienced.

In these dreams, there are three steps to the door where the woman is presented with her baby. I wonder if another pregnancy is planned. If she sees a gypsy woman in her dreams again, she should start clipping diaper coupons!

GIVING BIRTH TO KITTENS

I am now the busy mother of three, but when I was expecting my first child, I was pretty nervous. My husband and I had been married for four years and we had raised two cats from kittens. We kept them in the house and we really loved and spoiled them. Anyway, one night I dreamed that my delivery time had come, my husband rushed me to the hospital, and I gave birth to a kitten! In real life I had a beautiful little girl.

Giving birth to a household pet in a dream is not uncommon since for many of us a pet's birth may be the only live birth we have ever seen. As such it becomes a subconscious frame of reference. Cats are associated with femininity, a possible clue from the unconscious mind about the gender of the child.

ONE LAST CHILDLESS HURRAH

When I was about six months along in my pregnancy, I dreamed I had given birth to my baby. It was my husband's birthday, and family and friends were in our house. I was baking his cake; it was in the oven. I realized we didn't have any candles so I went to town to buy some. It was evening. I heard rock music coming out of a club and stopped in to listen. A band was playing on stage. They reminded me of the Doors. A very sexy lead singer wanted me to dance with him on stage. I did and it was very sexy and fun. Then I remembered the cake in the oven at home and I hurried back.

This dream reflects concerns about the changes in identity this woman will experience when she becomes a mother. As a mother, she may fear that her days of going out and having fun are over, but two-thirds of the way into her pregnancy there is no turning back. Many women experience a period of ambivalence during pregnancy. It is entirely rational to wonder, "what have I gotten myself into?" There are few things in life that can't be reversed or changed, but bringing a child into the world makes one a mother forever.

Her one last trip to town for candles indicates that she wonders if she is and will still be sexy after the baby comes. Her dream assures her that she is still desirable, since the sexy lead singer wants to dance with her on stage where everyone can watch. Since it is her husband's birthday, and the dream indicates she views this child as a gift to him, I sense he may have been a little more excited, at least initially, about the baby. Perhaps it was his idea to begin their family. I love the humor of her unconscious mind, with its "cake in the oven" reference (*cake* or *bun in the oven* being slang for pregnancy). She wonders how her body and life will change—normal concerns. Most moms do regain their figures. With the help of family and friends, she can manage and should arrange for some time alone with her husband after recovering from childbirth. A weekly date to look forward to can go along way toward reassuring her. Desires to hold onto sex appeal and some of the freedom of the childless life have creeped into this dreamer's vision. Understanding her anxieties will help her create a balanced life and avoid feeling resentful when the baby comes.

A MOTHER'S FEAR

After the caesarean delivery of my daughter and while still in the hospital, I had terrible nightmares that someone was in my room stealing or harming my baby.

A new mother often feels anxiety regarding the safety of her infant. After all, for nine months she kept him or her safe within the womb. Releasing a baby into the world makes it vulnerable. The natural maternal instinct to protect was surfacing with this dream. We have all heard terrible true stories of infants stolen from the hospital by someone posing as a nurse or other hospital employee, although, to be realistic, this happens very rarely. This dream reflects the natural desire to protect the child. While asleep, the new mother is oblivious to what is going on around her and would naturally feel vulnerable. But she shouldn't worry, she probably won't be getting too much sleep any time soon!

Having her infant kidnapped is a fear that crosses nearly every new mother's mind. The additional fear that, while asleep, she can't be attending to her baby is terrifying since she needs her sleep more than ever. Having loving helpers in attendance whenever possible can help a new mother get the rest she needs.

STAR BABY

I dreamed that I was pregnant and that there was much excitement and anticipation among my family and friends. Suddenly it occurred to me that I was not pregnant at all and I was concerned about having misled everyone. It turned out that actor John Goodman was supposedly the father of my child! So, I went to him, explained the predicament and told him we had to get busy, which we proceeded to do, so there would be a baby on the way.

Pregnancy in a dream is symbolic of a new creative project or idea the dreamer has conceived and is gestating or growing inside her. This dreamer has told everyone she has something new brewing, and then realizes it hasn't actually begun. The idea is there but the seeds are not planted. This dreamer may be inspired by the encouragement of others and therefore release the news before it actually is truth, to test the waters or gain support.

She wants the attention, support, and encouragement of friends and family, so she lets them believe that the project is further along than it actually is.

What does John Goodman represent to this dreamer? How would she describe him to someone who has never heard of him? The qualities that she would associate with John Goodman may be the ones the dreamer needs to create a new project. So, if she would describe Goodman as humorous, overweight, and loyal, her new idea or project requires her to use humor or a light approach, and that she be indulgent or lavish (overweight) when creating her project—do it in a big way! Her dream indicates that she should stick with her project through the ups and downs.

✳

A DREAM OF MY OWN BABY

I was thrilled when I learned I was pregnant. My husband and I had been infertile for seven years. But, while pregnant, a subconscious fear was revealed to me in a dream. I dreamed that I delivered a baby but it had the head of an old man. His face reminded me of Fred Mertz on *I Love Lucy!* He was bald, bossy, and grumpy. I was afraid that the baby would be born and then take over my life, that every thing would revolve around him or her, and that he or she would be very hard to please.

The truth was that my baby was fairly easy, although she *was* bald; and she hardly slept during the day—she seemed to want to take in everything around her. I envied other mothers whose infants would sleep through their banking, marketing, or other errands—not my sweet daughter! But she was, and is, the greatest joy of my life.

My dream did reveal a fear I hadn't consciously acknowledged. Once realizing it I was able to confront it and discuss it with other moms, including my sister who had delivered her first baby about ten months before me. This was exceptionally helpful.

IN ADDITION TO dreams reflecting fear of delivery, change of lifestyle, and the baby's health or appearance, other common pregnancy dream themes include feeling trapped in a confined area and swimming (after all, we begin life in a liquid environment). An expectant mother may fear the affect of her diet, drugs, alcohol, or even destructive emotions such as anger or jealousy on her unborn baby. Some women report beautiful and peaceful dreams in which they feel they have communicated with the baby inside them, dreaming of their gender, likes, and dislikes. Some dream of certain foods they would actually benefit from eating during this time.

Adding a child to your life does change everything, but it doesn't have to create anxiety and apprehension. Noting and interpreting your dreams will help you become aware of feelings you may be afraid to admit to yourself or others. New mothers may fear harsh judgment from others if they discuss their ambivalence toward motherhood or concerns about being a good mother. Motherhood is sacred in our society, and many of us worry about falling short of the expectations of our partner and family. So, once you are aware of your fears or self doubts, talk them over with a trusted advisor. A therapist, birthing coach, or other new mothers can relieve your fears. You are not alone. The very fact that you have concerns indicates that you have the qualities you need to be a good mother. What you don't know you can pick up. Learning your own dream-interpretation skills now will also help you in the future when your child begins to remember his or her own dreams. Listening to your child's dreams can help you understand their unconscious fears and motivations, and give you valuable clues to guide their development.

A s k   Y o u r s e l f

If you have dreams of being pregnant ask yourself these questions.

- If actually pregnant, what fears or concerns are revealed in my dream?
- If not actually pregnant, what new project do I want to create?

CHAPTER
SEVENTEEN

Dreams of Clothing

I n *dreams, clothing often represents the various roles* we play in life. New clothes may indicate that you have taken on a new image or role in life; old clothing may show that you are living with old ideas, and worn-out or old-fashioned roles. Wearing the opposite gender's clothing could mean that you are taking on some of the roles, activities, or qualities you associate with the other sex—or that you need to. Vintage or historical clothing relates to the relevant period and your own associations with this era. For some, it indicates a past-life memory. Pay attention to how you look and feel in the clothing you wear in your dreams—your feelings will offer clues to the meaning.

✳

A DIVORCED WOMAN STILL DREAMS
OF HER EX-HUSBAND

I have been divorced since 1993. In my dream, I came home after work to find my husband taking one of my favorite dresses out of the closet, and placing it on the floor with others. I ask him why, but before he can respond, a man I don't know comes out of another room with a vase of ours. He pays my husband some money for it (not very much) and, as he leaves, other people come out of other rooms with things they want to buy. When my husband sells a piece of Christmas china for fifty cents, I get very angry and make everyone leave. By the looks on their faces, I can tell that the people didn't realize that he was selling our things without my knowledge.

If clothing represents the roles we play in our lives, this dreamer's favorite dress represents the role of wife during the best and happiest of times. Her former husband shows his lack of respect for her with his actions in the dream by placing it on the floor. He further betrays her by selling the items she made her marriage nest with, and he undervalues them, too, as evidenced by the prices he charged for items special to her. In other words, he sells out!

The dreamer's focus on these betrayals indicates that she retains some resentment over the ending of the marriage. Since it has been many years since her divorce, she might benefit from some counseling to assist with her healing. Life is too precious to waste a day reliving regrets or resentments. Often, we don't honestly realize that we still carry these negative emotions. They can, however, have a profound effect on our lives, resulting in depression, anxiety, weight gain or loss, addiction, and other emotional and physical problems. Still, an individual may not connect the sadness from the past with current difficulties. Dreams may help make this connection known.

The Christmas plate in the dream is also important, because it represents traditions and rituals, special events and celebrations that help to define family life. The dreamer may resent the divorce most during these times. If she hasn't already, she would benefit from creating some new traditions of her own, focusing on the new creations rather than the way things used to be, or on what she no longer has. When we focus on past hurt, we remain victims. Even if we are entitled to be, it doesn't feel very good. This woman can start to reclaim her own life by creating a magical and beautiful holiday season for herself and those she loves.

A MAN DREAMS OF DRESSING LIKE A WOMAN

I assure you, I am a typical heterosexual male, but I have been having a dream that I find quite odd. I dream I am dressed in full female attire. I walk around and talk with nearly everyone I know! In another dream, I walked around the deck of a cruise ship; in a third, I was at work. It is not erotic. In the dreams I am extremely relaxed and feel as though this is or-dinary. No one else seems to notice or care. I always seem to have a pur-pose, somewhere to go and something to do.

Since no one else in this dream seems to notice or care, I believe this gentleman is being assured by his subconscious mind that it is perfectly fine to get in touch with or express more femi-nine qualities, especially when for an appropriate purpose. Clothing represents the roles we play in our lives, our uniforms, so to speak. This man should ask himself what qualities he associates with the female gender. Traditionally those would include nurturing, heal-ing, submissiveness—the softer, gentler opposite of the traditional male roles, which include provider, protector, and aggressor.

In this dream, people the man knows see him dressed as a woman and he carries on comfortably with his work and leisure life. The relaxed response suggests that his unconscious mind be-lieves all would be well if he took a more balanced approach to life. Some men get tired of holding up the stereotypical male persona at all times. Yet they fear that if they show any sensitivity or deviation from the manly man profile, others may get the wrong idea. Women also get tired of playing a role. They may act submissively with certain men or in certain situations in which they believe it is expected, even if it is not how they truly feel. Women in the 1950s were even encouraged to let their date or husband win at tennis! They were told not to express anger and to be dainty about the amount of food they ate when in the company of men. Men likewise were taught to appear confident, strong, and fearless even when they didn't necessarily feel that way.

Today, we recognize that both men and women experience all of the human qualities and emotions. Of course, there are differences between the sexes. The average man may be more assertive than the average woman. The average woman may be more nurturing than the average man. However, we all know exceptions to this within our own circle of acquaintances.

The healthiest way to live and interact is to get in touch with your true feelings and live as who you really are. I believe that this is what this dream depicts. I would suggest that this man try relaxing his image of manly behavior and see how he feels. It can be unsettling for a man to dream of dressing as a woman; some associate sexual and even deviant behavior with cross-dressing. However, this gentleman is being shown that if he tries a more feminine role or approach, the results will be fine.

THIS WOMAN DREAMS SHE IS MALE

In my dream, I was a male police officer. I was wearing the uniform, including the gun belt. I was driving a police car and was very aware that I needed to set a good example by the way I was driving. I had the sense that I wasn't a real officer and, if there was trouble, I would be inadequate to handle the situation appropriately.

Police are supposed to uphold and enforce the law; they can represent authority. It would seem that this woman has recently been put in a position of authority, something she doesn't feel altogether ready to accept or implement. This woman feels the need to take on her new position with a masculine approach. A title or new uniform does not automatically make you ready for the new responsibilities. She should make a list of what is expected of her and take inventory. If she needs to supplement her understanding or her abilities, she should seek classes or instruction that will give her the new skills she needs.

SOMETIMES, CLOTHING JUST sets the period of time. If you dream of clothing from other periods in history, ask yourself what you associate with that particular time. If the dream seems detailed and vivid, it may be a past life memory. Try to determine how the circumstances in your dream are affecting your life at this time. You could be repeating a pattern of lesson or instruction.

ONE MAN'S FANTASY—OR REALITY?

I have recently met and fallen in love with a man. I have known I was gay for at least ten years now, and have gone out with several guys, but I never knew I could love someone as deeply as I do Mark. In my dream, I am in a saloon. It seems to be the turn of the century. The room is decorated with ornately carved wood. There is a piano player in a striped shirt and vest. The bartender has a string tie and garters or leather ties around his sleeves at the upper arm. There is a beautiful woman in a blue dress with a very full skirt. I am wearing a suit and a hat, it looks fancy and dignified. I have an ascot at my neck. I am in love with the woman and when we kiss, well, I have never felt such a deep and blissful exchange. I woke up with the feeling of the kiss still on my lips.

Some say love is the most powerful force on the planet—that it can survive the grave and that it connects us in mysterious ways. It may be that this man's new love brought back a memory of a similar love in a past lifetime. Dreams that involve vintage clothing can be symbolic of the sensibilities of that particular period of history. Some would contend that when experienced in such detail, they could reflect a soul memory of a previous lifetime lived by the dreamer's soul. The majority of the people on the planet do believe in reincarnation, a philosophy that allows for the process of soul evolution through many lifetimes. The theory is that much like being in school, the soul continues to grow and learn, lifetime after lifetime, working on perfection or graduation. This dream may be reminding the dreamer that he has indeed known this wonderful deep love before. Wouldn't it be fascinating if the soul of his new lover was the soul of the woman in the dream, and they have re-united? A romantic notion, at the very least.

If you do believe in reincarnation, you will probably be a toler-ant and compassionate person since you may have been any eth-nicity or either gender along your soul's path. You may have been a bad guy one time and a good guy the next.

If this dreamer doesn't believe in reincarnation, then he could use the clothing in this dream as a symbol of its relevant period. What does the turn of the century bring to mind? How does he feel about that period and the roles that men and women played then? Does this particular period of history seem more conducive to ro-mance? What environment is ideal to cultivate and develop a love affair or relationship?

Whether reincarnation exists or not, the lessons learned from dreams of other periods can be enlightening and profound. Paying close attention to the clothing in our dreams can offer many helpful clues as to their meanings. Try to notice as many details as possible and log everything in your dream journal.

Ask Yourself

When interpreting the meaning of the clothing in your dreams, asking the following questions may be helpful.

- Do I recognize the clothing; does it have personal mean-ing?
- How do I feel about the clothing?
- Who would I imagine wearing this type of clothing?
- What adjectives would I use to describe the clothing?
- How do I feel about applying those same adjectives to myself?

Dreams of Teeth and Hair

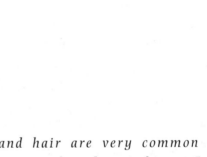

Dreams of teeth and hair are very common and typically relate to well-being, strength, and survival issues. In the animal kingdom, a creature that loses its teeth dies. Without these natural tools, it simply can no longer procure food, eat, or defend itself. Therefore, teeth dreams can relate to a concern for survival. They also relate to communication. If you need to make a decision and communicate that decision with someone—and you don't have all the information you need to make that decision—you may have a dream in which your teeth are loose or falling out. You don't have enough information to sink your teeth into the problem. Teeth can be an important part of appearance, and this may be a clue to what they mean in your dream. Of course, you may also have this dream theme if you have tooth pain, are overdue for a visit to the dentist, or grind your teeth in your sleep.

Hair has long been associated with strength, as in the Biblical story of Samson, who lost his might and powers when his hair was cut. Hair has had a purpose in spiritual and sacred matters as well. Lovers carry a lock of their beloved's hair to keep them close at heart. Mothers save the first lock of hair cut from their child's head as a souvenir of the momentous event. Hair is also associated with sexuality, virility, seduction, health, and power.

JUST CALL ME SMOOTH GUMS

For a period of years I had a frequent and incredibly vivid dream that all my teeth were falling out. Usually I could feel them in my mouth like a handful of Chiclets, as I slowly spat them out one by one. I dreamed that I could feel the smooth gumline where my teeth once were. The tooth loss never seemed to be in response to anything, I wasn't hit in the mouth or suffering tooth decay.

This is a surprisingly common dream theme. Teeth represent healthy survival. In a more modern context, losing teeth also refers to losing power or grasp on a situation. Perhaps this dreamer didn't have all of the information he needed to decide how he felt. The dreamer may have felt ineffective about his ability to communicate, or he may have felt powerless in another way. When something changed in his life to help empower him, or he gained understanding of his life's circumstances and felt more in control, he stopped having the dream.

CLEAN-SHAVEN SANTA

In my dream, my surprised wife asked what happened? And I said they trimmed my beard for a movie. Then I went to work at the galleria, where I am Santa Claus. Everyone was disappointed. It was then I realized my beard was cut too short and my chin was bare. I was heartsick. I knew it would take five months for it to grow back. Then I woke up and was relieved to feel my beard still there. By the way, I do work as Santa at the mall.

This dreamer obviously enjoys his role as Santa Claus very much and doesn't want to disappoint anyone. A beard is an integral part of Santa's appearance and of the dreamer's own identity. His mild fear of not measuring up is demonstrated in the dream as the loss of it. Although numbers in dreams are often very significant, the five-month period in this dream seems of importance, mainly because it will take him way out of the holiday season, preventing Mr. Claus from doing the work he loves, at least for this year. Since he doesn't consider wearing a fake beard as a replacement, the dream indicates he has an authentic, genuine dedication to this role. Beards can hide a face, or act as a disguise, but here they make the man magic!

✳

NEW HAIR

As a man heading into his mid-thirties, I occasionally dream of being bald and trying desperately to hide it. However, last night I dreamed I had a beautiful, thick head of hair! It reached down to my shoulder blades and I felt quite pleased. In this dream I was wearing a finely tailored suit. Friends were commenting on the suit and the hair, saying how much they liked both. As I left that scene, I wandered into a parking garage. I got into a large classic Lincoln from the 1950s and drove away.

Hair is associated with strength, sexuality, virility, seduction, health, and power. Previous dreams that depicted this man as bald and trying to cover it up may have occurred when he felt insecure about his strength or sex appeal. In this case, he is confident in his appearance and valued by others. He makes quite an impression. The large classic Lincoln, like the man in his long hair and suit, is sure to get positive attention. I suspect that the recent events in his waking life gave him cause to feel confident and proud, and his dream just pointed that out to him. He's the man!

Bald can be beautiful, too, but this dreamer seems to associate long healthy hair with being successful and well liked. Yet the actual life events that prompted the dream could have been unrelated to appearance. He may have received a raise or praise from his boss or a woman he was attracted to may have agreed to a date. Anything that enhanced his sense of self-worth may have triggered this dream.

MORE TEETH

I have a recurring dream in which my teeth are falling out. It is so vivid that I wake myself and have to feel my teeth to make sure they are still there. Until I am fully awake I feel as though they are loose. Of course they are not falling out, but I have had this dream occasionally for many years.

This dream of teeth loss is so vivid that the dreamer actually needs a reality check when she wakes up! She should ask herself where in her life there is a similar fear of loss. Is she aware of any anxiety that she keeps just below the surface? Any area where she feels a bit insecure could be the cause.

When dreams are so vivid that you don't know what is real until you are fully awake, they are certainly saying, "this is important, pay attention!" Since this dream is recurring, I wonder if the dreamer often regrets saying something. Loose teeth may be the same as loose lips. If she does tend to regret speaking too quickly, she could try to be aware of her thoughts in advance and choose more carefully. No one wants to put a foot in their mouth!

If this dream is familiar, take a look at the chapter on recurring dreams as well.

ASK YOURSELF

If you dream of losing your teeth or hair ask yourself the following questions.

- What fear is surfacing at this time?
- Have I said something I regret?
- Am I fearful of any survival issue: paying the bills, health concerns, a challenging relationship?
- Do I need more information regarding something about which I am making a decision?
- Have I recently changed my appearance or am I concerned about my looks?

Dreams of
Purses, Wallets, and Money

P urses and wallets hold our identification. They can represent who we are, or at least who we represent ourselves to be. A purse also holds cosmetics, medication, and money—likewise a wallet may contain I.D., a driver's license, business and credit cards. Losing either in a dream may indicate that you are losing yourself in a relationship or that you are in a life circumstance, such as losing a job, that robs you of title and income. Or it could signify losing a relationship to death or divorce. Even a child going away to college can invoke feelings of changing identity. If you find a purse or wallet in your dream, you may be trying to change your identity or how others see you. Spend some time writing about yourself and answering the following questions. What is important to you? What do you believe in? What are your goals? In short, who are you?

As distinct from purses and wallets, money can represent something we value and it is often associated with self-worth. If abundant in supply, you feel good about yourself and your resources, financial and otherwise. If scarce, you may feel depleted or undervalued. Money also represents energy, barter, motivation, and reward. So, finding money in your dream may be a personal reward from your subconscious mind, telling you that you are doing a good job. It could also indicate that you will stumble upon something of personal value. What you then find could be a bit of philosophy that you find helpful, a loving expression from a friend, or something else valuable. Or you may, as you will see in the dreams in this section, actually find or win cash!

LOST HANDBAG

For many years, sometimes four or more times each year, I have the same unpleasant dream. I discover my handbag containing cash, credit cards, driver's license, and so on, has disappeared. I experience a dreadful feeling of anxiety. In desperation, I retrace my steps in search of the missing handbag but to no avail. At this point, I wake up and my relief is tremendous!

Handbags, purses, and wallets represent our identity in dreams, our I.D. Without cash, credit cards, and identification, we are pretty much powerless in modern society. Hence, this dream reflects those times in the dreamer's life when she is experiencing a bit of an identity crisis: Who am I? Where am I powerful? This dreamer could be a woman who doesn't have a strong sense of self. She may go along in life conforming to what she thinks others expect of her. When that is not enough, and she loses a relationship or job, she will feel as though she needs to retrace her steps, asking herself, "Where did it all go wrong?" However, going backward doesn't recover the handbag, or who she is. Next time she experiences this dream, she should take a little time to define herself. A strong sense of self and reinforcing one's personal values can prevent this from happening.

Answering these critical questions can help: Who am I? What is important to me? How many hats am I wearing at present? We all play many roles in our lives—worker, adult, child, sibling, friend, classmate, and so on. Sometimes, we lose track of what is really important to us. Writing her answers in a journal should reinforce her definition of self and help her hold on to it during busy times in the future.

✳

EMPTY PURSE

I was in an attorney's office and, when I came out, I had forgotten my purse. Someone ran after me with the purse but, when I took hold of it, it was light. I looked inside and it was completely empty! I ran to the window and looked out to the street to see if my car was still there. It had disappeared as well. I was very concerned about someone getting into my house since my keys were in the purse. I tried to call the police but was given an instrument that looked like an old fashioned horn-style hearing aid. Needless to say, no help was forthcoming.

Maybe this dreamer feels robbed by an attorney who cleaned her out! Hopefully not, but she does seem to feel that she is in danger of losing everything, and that there is very little help to be found. Perhaps she has just gone through a divorce or other life-changing experience, such as a change of profession. Her dream indicates that the way in which she defines herself has changed. A purse represents our I.D. In other words, her identity, who she is and how she presents herself to the world. Her car theft is significant, too, for cars and other vehicles represent our bodies, since the body is the vehicle of the spirit and consciousness. She also worries about her home being invaded, which is interesting, since homes can also represent the physical body.

The police or authorities aren't able to help in this situation. In fact, they offer only old-fashioned assistance. It appears that this loss is something she will have to handle alone. This is a great time for her to decide who she is, what she stands for, and how she wants the world to know her. She may also feel betrayed by those who should be helpful during this time of change. If this is the case, she should seek out loving and supportive people who can comfort her through this process. Even though she must make these changes or choices alone, she does not need to be without support from people who have her best interests at heart.

FOUND MONEY!

I have been having this dream for the last couple of years. I always find money on the floor, and lots of it. I put it away in my drawer or the pocket of my trousers. Since the dream is so real, I sometimes look for it when I wake up, but it is not there, of course. I always wake up feeling good, thinking I will find some money that day.

Money represents all sorts of things we value, which could include actual cash. The question is, does this dreamer find money the day he wakes up from the dream? If not, it could be a sign that he will come across other things he values, such as time with a dear friend, a stock tip, even some creative inspiration. In the dream, he puts the money away. Has he put money away for his future? It may be that his unconscious mind is reminding him to invest in an IRA, or other retirement account. In any case, waking up feeling good is a good sign! There may be hidden treasures to discover in the day following such a dream.

The floor—what we stand on—is our foundation, and can represent our values. Finding money on the floor might be a reward for taking a positive stand. The floor is also below our average range of vision; we have to look down to see it. Perhaps the dreamer is being told to keep his vision on his values to reap real rewards.

ONLY WEARING A PURSE

When I had this dream, my boyfriend and I had just broken up and my heart had been broken. I was at a museum, naked except for a purse with its strap slipping from my shoulder. I started walking home. Strangers nonchalantly commented, "Do you realize your purse strap is off your shoulder?" They were unconcerned about my nakedness. My ex drove by in an old Chevy with other guys. They stopped, but when I asked for a ride they said they were going the opposite way. My ex got out and walked me home politely. He, too, was oblivious to my nakedness, though he did point out that my purse strap was off my shoulder.

Museums display valuable items from the past, which makes it the perfect location for this woman to review what she valued from her relationship. Being naked, in this case, indicates that she was stripped of all protection that came with the role she played, a result, no doubt, of her recent breakup. So, there she is her true vulnerable self, carrying a purse—her identity, the version of herself that she wants to present to the world. Hers keeps falling off her shoulder: Now that she is no longer half of a couple, the way she presents herself has changed.

The old Chevy again refers to the past. The relationship is over and she and her boyfriend are headed in different directions. The fact that no one, including her ex, notices her nakedness could mean that she believes he no longer finds her sexually attractive—or that he accepts her honest and vulnerable presence as normal. Her ex does notice that her identity has changed and walks her home politely, indicating that she feels he tried to do things the right way.

Stripped of her role as girlfriend, this dreamer takes a naked and honest look at the situation. She holds on to her sense of self . . . still having her purse with her. She seems like a very healthy person going through a difficult time. She will heal and move on, without a doubt.

✳

WINNING MONEY

In my dream, a guy told me to bet only on horses at the fifth post. The next day, at the Pick Six at the racetrack, every horse that ran from the fifth post won! A few weeks later, I dreamed that Park Royal won the race and paid $13.50 for a $2.00 bet. That came true. The night before I went to Reno, I dreamed I won the jackpot. I played the slots when I got there and won three jackpots in twenty-four hours. Am I tapping into something here?

It seems that this fellow is plugged in to the big pit boss in the sky. Since he is winning, my advice is—carry on! He should just be sure never to gamble more than he can afford to lose.

Gambling in a dream can be positive or negative, based on the context of the dream. You could be encouraged to take a risk, especially if you tend to be too conservative for your own good. Or you could be shown negative results from gambling to demonstrate that the risk is not worth taking. Numbers are often significant, and can be representative of important things to the dreamer such as a birthdate, an address, or a time. So, this man could ask himself if the numbers one, three, five, or zero have any special meaning to him. But, in this case, the dreams seem pretty literal.

Many people dream of winning or making an important business decision. Author and financial educator Suze Orman says that she woke one morning with the title, *The Courage To Be Rich.* She went on to write this best-selling book, which helps people change their thoughts about money and create wealth. Before approaching the *Los Angeles Times* about writing a dream interpretation column for them, I actually dreamed an entire column. I have also dreamed chapters and titles and even invented a game. Paying attention to your dreams can become very profitable.

ASK YOURSELF

If you have dreams containing a purse, wallet, or money, ask yourself these questions.

- Have I recently changed the way I define myself or the roles I play in my life?
- Do I feel that I have lost myself in too much work, an overwhelming relationship, or a major change?
- Am I looking for a new identity?
- Am I questioning my values?
- Do I need to pay more attention to my financial situation?

Dreams of House and Home

$\mathcal{S}$ince *your body is the home of your spirit, mind,*
and soul, a house in your dream can represent your physical body.
The structure of the house is also symbolic. The basement, for example, may represent your subconscious mind, what is below the
surface; the staircase could represent your spine, the steps that
climb from the basement to the attic; the front door, your heart; the
main floors, your conscious mind or what you are aware of and
thinking about; and the attic, your mind and your superconscious
or overself, an aspect that may offer spiritual enlightenment or
guidance.

The various rooms may also represent more literally the
activities that take place there. So, the kitchen could stand for nutrition and dietary concerns; the bathroom, cleansing and releasing
of what you no longer need; the bedroom, rest, sleep, privacy, sex,
recuperation from illness.

Your childhood home may come into your dream to represent

what you learned during childhood, to evoke certain feelings, or to express other childhood concerns that are still influencing your life. The home where you lived during your formative years can appear when you are rethinking something from that time or are gaining a new adult perspective on what went on then. Home, especially the childhood home, is associated with security; it should be a safe place, however, for many it isn't.

Naturally, if you are involved in buying, building, or remodeling a home, your dream may be entirely about these events. Though exciting, these major life changes can be stressful. You may be working through the stress or even getting decorating ideas in your dreams! Always begin any dream interpretation with the literal or obvious meaning before looking for deeper understanding.

Of course, your own personal associations with your home are important to consider as well. Your feelings about your home, the activities you are involved in there, and who you share your home with may all be significant elements in understanding your dream.

CHOOSING A HOME

In my recurring dream, the details vary but the gist is the same. I am in a house that is divided into two separate living sections, upstairs and downstairs, as in a duplex apartment. The surroundings are familiar to me. It is on the ocean. Each of the two living quarters has its own benefits. One has easier access to the ocean; the other has more light and is more spacious. I always feel as if I am torn about which to claim as my space, or that I have already made a choice and it is the wrong one. What does this mean?

This dream depicts a conflict between two parts of the self. One part wants to be above it all, in the upper apartment, where the dreamer has space and light, which are symbolic of solitude, spiritual enlightenment, and peace. Downstairs, she is closer to the ocean, symbolic of emotion and the unconscious. This dreamer may feel she has to choose between being a more spiritually concerned person and a more physical and emotional one. The good news is that in truth none of us has to choose. Understand that these are both real parts of you. Sometimes, we need to be alone with our thoughts. Other times we need to be in the surf, feeling and experiencing all that life has to offer. I would suggest that this dreamer imagine an elevator connecting the two apartments and decide to live in both. The anxiety comes from denying a part of herself, and there is no need to do this. She doesn't need to be one or the other. Acknowledging both the spiritual and the physical parts of herself will help her to integrate these aspects.

WHO IS IN MY HOUSE?

I am in my home (not my actual home) and I go from room to room and everything is familiar. People I don't know start coming into my home uninvited. They help themselves to my food and drink and talk among themselves. I ask them to leave, but no one pays attention to me. I get frantic trying to get everyone to leave my home. I end up screaming at them, "Get out of my house!" No one does. I woke up feeling disturbed.

This dreamer feels invisible and mute, invaded by uninvited interruptions and others who make demands on her. She will benefit from creating focused intentions and not giving up until she is heard and seen. Her resources nurture these people but they ignore her requests. Somewhere in her life she is not being taken seriously. Who isn't listening? She feels like she's communicating, she is making a real effort, but it is not effective. Who ignores her? First, she should try to discover who the takers are in her life.

Next, this dreamer should examine ways in which she may not actually be assertive enough and try to improve her communication skills. If she doesn't correct this situation her resentment will build. (She already feels like screaming.) She seems like a very nice woman who doesn't want to hurt the feelings of others. She is expressing herself, but others don't hear her words the same way she means them. Being polite is a good thing, but she could still be clear and direct in her communication.

Now, as with most dreams, there is more than one possible interpretation. Here are my other thoughts. If this dreamer has a weight problem or an eating disorder, these people who eat and ignore her in her dream could be the addictive forces that drive her to eat and that she can't seem to control. If this is the case, I would suggest talking her weight issues over with her physician or psychologist. With help she can take back control of her body and her life.

＊

MY DOOR WON'T CLOSE!

I understand that a house can represent one's body. My recurrent dream has me unable to make my door stay closed. Although I lock the door and repeatedly slam it to get it to latch, the door opens easily, causing me concern.

Doors in the language of dreams can represent new opportunities or a transition into a new state of being. In the metaphor of the house, the door may represent the heart. So I ask this dreamer if he is willing to open his heart to a new opportunity for love or a transition in matters of the heart? Since he slams the door shut and locks it, he may have been hurt and is now protecting himself. Just like a child who touches a candle flame, once hurt we are often very resistant to making ourselves vulnerable again. Apparently, his unconscious mind wants him to be open to new possibilities. Since the door opens easily, perhaps he is fearful that he will fall in love too easily, or is too accepting. If he has lost himself in relationships, he should redefine and reinforce his sense of self and venture on. We can learn from past pain to protect ourselves and still be available to love.

WHERE DO I BELONG?

My recurring dream involves confusion about where I live. There is some problem with the house I am living in, and I feel I am only renting it. I am confused because I know I own a house but I am not living in it.

Renting is usually temporary, so, since the dreamer owns her home, this is a confusing dream image. Some people believe that the body is the temporary or rented house for your spirit or soul and that you may leave your body while sleeping to spend time in the world of spirit. During these times you may remember other homes or bodies your spirit has occupied. This serves a purpose, an opportunity to grow and to learn lessons.

The dreamer may be describing the confusion the spirit feels after it leaves the body during sleep and then returns. This experience can take other forms, such as not being able to find your car (vehicles being symbolic of the body since the body is the vehicle for the spirit). Others simply can't find their way home and feel lost.

If this is a new concept to you, you should know that we always come home to our body, no matter how far we travel. Our spirits are attached to our bodies with what has been described by many spiritual leaders as a *silver cord*. This cord is never severed until the moment the physical body dies and the spirit is free to move on.

DISCOVERING MORE ROOMS

I was in my house, but at the top of the stairs there was a door or a hallway that I had never noticed before. Beyond the hallway there were more rooms. In the rooms were great and beautiful things, including old and fabulous objects like those I have found among my grandmother's things—beautiful antique clothing, furnishings, and the like. It is so odd and amazing that I had never noticed this hallway and all the additional rooms and good stuff waiting for me!

This is one of the most common dream themes—people discovering new rooms, areas, and objects within their own homes. They are always amazed by this discovery and it is nearly always pleasant. This dream may indicate that the dreamer has recently discovered that there is more to her than she knew, more dimension previously unseen. She may have recently found new reserves of courage or patience, for example. Since many of the things she discovers are old-fashioned, it could be that she is opening up to a past-life memory, or simply to the memory of her grandmother and her influence. Either way, she has hidden resources that, once realized with the help of her dream, she can count on.

✳

ANOTHER VARIATION ON THIS THEME

I have this dream a lot. I am always in an empty house. Sometimes it is a house that I know from the past, other times it is new to me. Usually the house is empty and dark. It is often dusty and unlived in. I throw open the windows, paint the walls, and bring in furnishings. Often, I discover rooms I didn't know were there. The rooms are usually filled with old things, such as bicycles and birdcages. Sometimes there are old clothes that I try on. One room can lead to another. I feel anticipation, curiosity, and sometimes a mild sense of fear as I explore new chambers in what seems like endless space.

It sounds to me like this dreamer is reviewing past lives and possibly visiting future ones in his sleep! The empty and dark house could be an unoccupied body or life. The old things he finds are mementos of past times and lives. Either that or he is reviewing his own past in this lifetime and his future as well. Bicycles are a self-powered form of transportation, which require careful balance. Birdcages represent limits and feeling trapped, but these are empty, left behind. The old clothes he tries on could also indicate a review of the roles he has played in past times. Then he looks to the future to discover what lies ahead in "new chambers in what seems like endless space."

We do often take time to review where we are and what we are doing. In the sleep state our spirit is free to check in, review, and make plans for the future. Life is unlimited. It seems that this dreamer is often involved in a healthy review and in planning for the future.

Repairing or sprucing up a house may indicate a need to do the same to his physical body. Cleaning the house may suggest a cleansing fast or some attention to diet and digestion. Opening windows can mean to open his eyes and take a good look. Does he want to live in the past or present? Is he seeing his world accurately? He can bring the good that he has learned forward, live in the now, and plan for the future!

DREAMS OF CHILDHOOD HOME ✶

Anytime that I have a dream it takes place in the home I lived in from the ages of ten through twenty-five, but the people in the dream are from the present. Since leaving that house, I have lived in six different places. However, my dreams never take place in any of those homes.

Dreams that take place in a childhood home often reflect the principles we learned in those formative years. They can represent a desire for the security of our youths when we had less responsibility, or we were dependent on our family. They may also refer to situations that took place at that time, and are resurfacing to be better understood from an adult perspective. I would ask this dreamer what his strongest memories are from the period of his life between ten and twenty-five. What issue is cycling through his psyche now that began then? To get in touch with the message of this dream, the dreamer might take pencil and paper and collect any mementos from that time. Perhaps a childhood toy or photograph could be found. If there is music that the dreamer associates with this period, that would also be very helpful to listen to during this exercise. Once the setting is complete, the dreamer should close his eyes for a few moments and relax, taking a few deep breaths to aid relaxation. The questions the dreamer should ask include:

- What are my strongest memories from my tenth to my twenty-fifth year?
- What change occurred at age ten?
- What change happened at age twenty-five?
- What does that period of time mean to me?
- What does that old house remind me of?

MY OWN BASEMENT DREAM

I once had a dream in which there was a door to the basement from my bedroom. The basement was on the same level and had an earth floor. In it there were dead bodies neatly stacked like wood logs. I didn't want my daughter to see this bizarre and grisly scene, for I was afraid that she wouldn't understand it.

Even the most weird or grisly depiction in a dream can have a beautiful meaning once we try to understand it. My interpretation of this one is that the dead bodies stored in my basement are influences of those who have been important in my life. I keep them neatly organized in my subconscious mind, although they continue to influence my life. I pay tribute to them by keeping them close. As an avid reader I love the work of many philosophers and thinkers, and I believe that they are the bodies I keep in my basement. In life, I want my daughter to discover her own truth and philosophy. I have tried hard not to influence her too much, but rather ask her to think for herself. Of course, I also expose her to great teachers, but I encourage her to decide for herself how she feels. This could explain why I didn't want her to see what was stored in my basement closet. The earth floor to me means that these great teachers are my foundation and what keeps me grounded.

A s k Y o u r s e l f

If you have dreams of houses, ask yourself these questions.

- How did I feel in the home in my dream?
- What did the home remind me of?
- What elements of the home stood out?
- In what ways does the dream home relate to my current home?
- Does it make sense to use the dream home as a metaphor for my body?
- What can I learn from this dream?

Dreams of Hotels

Dreams of hotels, motels, lodges, and other vacation dwellings can indicate a need for the dreamer to get away to gain perspective, rest, and relaxation. These places can also indicate that the dreamer is dealing with a temporary situation, since each is a transient lodging place.

*

VACATION IN MY DREAMS

I frequently dream that I am in a hotel. The dream itself and my activities in the dream vary. The consistent aspect is that I am somewhere in some sort of a hotel. I might be in the room, the hallway, the lobby, and so on. I dream at least once a week of being in a hotel and, often, more frequently. I only travel three or four times a year, and don't spend much time in hotels, so this baffles me.

It would seem that this dreamer considers much to be temporary in her life. Relationship, career, even where she lives, could be symbolized by this dream. Hotels are temporary dwelling places and, as such, they are symbolic of a temporary situation. The rest of the dream will offer many clues to the larger meaning. The lobby is a very public place and could mean that she is temporarily in the public eye, or feels that others are aware of her activities. The hallway, which gets you from one place to another, may indicate a transition, move, or change. The room indicates a temporary need for rest. Since this is a frequent recurring theme, the dreamer should ask what in her life feels temporary? Where does she want to make changes? It could be that she needs to create change—or stability, depending on the specific details!

UNCLOTHED!

In my dream I'm in my bed waking up—only it isn't my bed. It isn't my room. It's a strange hotel room. Under the bedclothes I'm naked. I peer around. No suitcase. No clothes of any kind. I know I've got to be somewhere this morning to teach a seminar, but where? It will damage my reputation if I'm a no-show. My heart thuds. What should I do? Should I wrap myself in the bedspread? Patter down to the lobby and fling myself on the mercy of the desk clerk? Then I really wake up. I'm in my own room with a closet full of clothes only a few yards away.

The hotel room is a temporary resting place, just a quick event in your life. The fact that it's strange to this dreamer indicates that he doesn't feel this way often. Nudity in our dreams means that we are being honest, not covering up anything. However, since he needs to be somewhere and doesn't have his clothing, he is unprepared, without the professional attitude or appearance necessary. He can't play the right role without the proper attire.

"Heart thud" indicates an emotional awareness. Even in the dream, he is concerned about his reputation! The dream indicates a mild anxiety about the way the dreamer is perceived professionally. He wants to be himself, but may feel that he needs to cover up some aspects of self to be considered properly. Should he go to an authority figure (desk clerk), hope to win their assistance, and risk being exposed? I would suggest that he consider the situation and what exactly he wants to accomplish or communicate. Sometimes it isn't appropriate or necessary to reveal all in the workplace. If his view could upset things and there is really no reason to risk this, keep it covered up! If the dream persists, he could try writing his truths, or what he risks exposing, in a journal.

ASK YOURSELF

If you have dreams of hotels, ask yourself the following questions.

- What feels or is temporary in my life at this time?
- Do I need some rest and relaxation?
- Have I been too social lately, needing some space?
- What comes to mind when I think of hotels?
- Am I trying to get away from something?

Dreams of Vehicles

Planes, trains, and automobiles—in fact, any vehicle—can represent the physical body, since the body is the vehicle for the spirit and the mind. Old-fashioned transportation can then indicate a sense that the body is behind the times, out of shape, or moving more slowly than it used to. A bicycle or motorcycle requires balance, so the interpretation might be that you require more careful balance in your daily life. Since the ocean can represent emotion, a boat can keep you close to—but just above—feeling emotion. A bus, on the other hand, may mean that many are going along with you, or the characters on the bus may all be depictions of the many facets of your personality.

If you are a passenger, you are going along for the ride, but not in control of your path, unless you have hired a chauffeur. If driving, you are making the choices and in control. If the vehicle is out of control, check your nutrition, addictions, and stress level. If you are going uphill, maybe it is tough but you are moving upward toward your goals. If headed downhill, you may be sliding backward or taking the easy way out. Note the make and color of the vehicle for other clues.

MOTORCYCLE

I'm thirty-two years old. For as long as I can remember, I have had the same dream about once a month. I am riding my motorcycle along the edge of a very beautiful but deep canyon. I am not panicked at all; I just go along enjoying the ride. Then, for no reason, I suddenly ride off the cliff. I wake up before I crash at the bottom.

The motorcycle in this dream indicates that the dreamer lives his life in a balanced way even though he seems to like being on the edge. What would be frightening to most doesn't faze him. In fact, he appreciates the beauty of this precarious position. Understanding both sides of any situation gives one balance and confidence in life. Many are too afraid to take the risks in their lives that would aid them in getting what they really want. This man is not afraid—in fact, even when something goes wrong, he survives. This indicates to me that when something doesn't go as planned, he picks himself up, dusts himself off, figures out what he can learn from the experience, and moves on. The only danger is that if he is addicted to risk and high drama, he may get bored easily, require constant change, have trouble committing to a romantic relationship, or feel dissatisfied with a job that doesn't challenge him. However, the dream indicates that he can find the balance required to have a satisfying life.

DRIVE OVER A CLIFF

I'm driving through a canyon and the sun is shining after days of rain. I am happily listening to music when a sharp turn appears and I hit my brakes. I hear wheels screech until I go smoothly over the cliff. At that moment it is completely silent, and I think to myself, this is it, it's my time. I verbalize I love you to my family and think how blue the water looks. I see the pebbles on the shore getting closer, but tell myself it won't hurt. Upon impact all is quiet and I am in a yellowish nothingness.

I then wake up out of breath, my teeth numb, and unable to move momentarily. Since two of my past dreams, trivial but vivid, have come true, this one is disturbing to me. Could it be a premonition?

The spiritual and symbolic nature of this dream reassures me that it is not a premonition. If this dreamer thinks back to the dreams she has had that came true, my bet is, she will remember that they felt different than this one, probably shorter in duration and more literal.

This dream reflects the symbolic road of life and asks the dreamer not to become complacent, to be alert to sudden changes, and be ready to react. The spiritual interpretation is quite beautiful, telling her that when her time does come, "after days of rain" or many emotional experiences, there will be a cleansing. This will happen further down the road and, since she decides to "hit the brakes" or stop moving forward, she will be in control. Sharing love with family is the most urgent request of dying patients and the most desired experience for those left behind.

The ocean is associated with returning to God. Using the ocean then, as a metaphor for the enormity of the Creator, each individual could be represented by a small portion—say, a sand pail full of water from the ocean. When we die, it is said that our soul or spirit returns to its home with the heavenly parent and, as such, we are returned to our source.

The ocean is often used in this metaphor because it is full of living creatures that are nourished and grow in its environment. Just like human bodies, the bodies of the animals who live in the ocean are mostly water. So, the creatures there are made of the same stuff as the environment they live in and that sustains them. In the same way, on the spiritual level of existence, it is said that our spirits live in the Great Spirit our creator, who provides everything we need.

In this dream, it appears that she will reach the water as her car sails over the cliff. The color blue, which she remarks on, is often associated with spirituality. The "yellow nothingness" refers to the mental or conscious state that remains after the body is no longer alive.

The physical sensations this woman experienced after the dream show that she was very physically involved in this dream. She was no doubt holding her breath, clenching her teeth, and tightening her muscles as she hit the water in her mental movie and, when she woke, she still felt the result of this experience. So, to reassure her, hers is a dream that confirms that she will have a long, productive life and, when the time comes, all her affairs will be in order and she will leave this life feeling content.

Many dreamers are concerned that a vivid dream they have experienced will come true, but dreams of our own death are nearly always symbolic of the ending of one state of being and the beginning of another, not of actual physical death. Graduating from college, for example is the end or death of life as a student and the birth of life as a working member of society. That sort of situation could spawn this dream.

*

NO CONTROL

I have this recurring dream that I can't understand. I am driving my car and I can't seem to put my foot on the brake. My foot is not on the gas either, yet the car is motion (sometimes fast, sometimes slow). I never dream of an accident, but my feet are jumbled up on the seat and I just can't seem to make the car stop. I am hoping you can explain this to me.

In dreams, all vehicles can represent us as we go through our lives. So, here, even though she is at the wheel she is not really in control of her life. It would seem that she can't stop what she is doing, that somehow she is ineffective, she may feel impatient or impotent. She is steering or determining the direction she takes in her life but can't seem to control the speed. Something outside of her immediate control governs how fast or slowly she proceeds. Feet can represent our foundation, balance, and what we stand for. Since hers are "jumbled up" and can't be used properly, perhaps the dream suggests that she take a stand and take back control of her life or situation.

LOST CAR

For the last two years, I have had a recurring dream of losing my car. The scenes are different but the end result—that I am looking for my car—is the same. In the beginning, I was very upset when I lost my car but now I am more relaxed about it, although still mildly affected.

The feeling of having lost our way is a common one. Many dreamers report not being able to find their car or their street or their home in a dream. If you experience this, try to determine what you have lost in your waking life or how far from your destination you are. You may want to draw yourself a map so that it doesn't happen again. A life map could be created by writing down your purpose and goals, and then the steps or roads that lead there. You can also do this in collage form by cutting out pictures from magazines that illustrate your goals, and gluing them to a piece of cardboard that you can keep within daily view.

Perhaps this dreamer is off her path! Each of us comes into this life with a specific purpose, something to accomplish or learn. We also have something to offer as our gift to the world we are born into to. When we get off our path, there is discomfort. The longer and farther away we are from this path or purpose, the more unsettled we may feel. We are away from "home," off base, and we feel lost. Another way that people describe this feeling is to say that something is missing. They can have dreams of looking, searching, and not finding what it is that seems lost. In their waking life they feel unfulfilled and discontent. There is an underlying feeling that they have forgotten something important, but they have no idea what that something could be.

Often this dissatisfaction permeates the person's life in general, and a mild depression or anxiety can result. We all know that this is true! Think about a time when you have had a specific purpose. It could be anything—let's say you are planning a vacation. You make the decision, you and your husband will go to Hawaii the last week of August. You envision sunsets, mai tais, exotic women in hula skirts, snorkeling, a perfect week of rest and relaxation. You are planning a trip and this is your purpose, your mission. If, during this time, a minor setback occurs, you take it in stride. Say you get a parking ticket outside the travel agent's office. "Shoot!" you say, but then you think, "Oh well, soon I will be basking in the sun in paradise! So what? I will consider this a contribution to the local police, they work hard and I did miss the *no parking* sign. It is no big deal."

You are enthusiastic, involved in life, and excited, anticipating the future in a positive way. So it is with knowing your life purpose. Everything that comes along either fits or doesn't fit into your path. But when you are not feeling on track, every minor setback becomes fuel for the feeling of discontent.

Finding your life purpose is not difficult; just start by looking to your natural skills, talents, and abilities. What do you feel drawn to? What causes do you feel pulled toward? These will all offer clues. Some people believe that their life purpose must be something huge. This is often not the case. Some will be determined to find a cure for a disease, discover a distant planet, negotiate world peace, but most of us will accomplish our purpose within our own universe. Your purpose could be forgiveness—that is, to be forgiving and to be an example to others of this gracious attitude. Maybe your life purpose is to be peaceful, giving others a feeling of calm and well being just by being in your presence. Maybe you raise well-adjusted and positive children who, in turn, make the world a better place. Find your purpose and live in accordance with it and you will never feel lost.

Another explanation of this dream may take suspending disbelief, but many people are convinced that the spirit leaves the body during sleep. Since the body is the vehicle of the spirit, it may be that the dreamer's spirit is just returning to her body and is temporarily "lost." Many people have variations of this dream. So, this could be a dream in which she is astral projecting, leaving the confines of the physical body to explore other areas and then just looking for her way back to her body. There may be a vague memory of the process and that could inspire this dream.

BOYFRIEND CAN'T HIT THE BRAKES

My boyfriend and I are moving in together next month. He dreamed that we were driving down a winding road when he realized the brakes wouldn't work. He managed to drive into some bushes and stop. Is he afraid of the commitment?

Good question and reasonable concern, but this boyfriend's dream isn't about commitment so much as fear of the unknown. Major life changes are often accompanied by dreams of warning. Here, it would appear that the boyfriend is naturally concerned about how their relationship will change once the couple lives together.

When driving on a winding road (their new life path together), it is impossible to see around the bend. He doesn't know what to expect as they make this change. He has committed to the new arrangement, and feels he can't really stop. He is experiencing very normal concerns about how the new living arrangement will affect the relationship. He probably just doesn't want to lose the good thing he feels he has with his girlfriend now.

She can reassure him by making living together even better than their relationship has been so far! If each of them is able to continue separate activities as well as joint ones, they should do fine.

A S K   Y O U R S E L F

If you have dreams about vehicles ask yourself these questions.

- What is the vehicle and how do I relate to it?
- Have you owned or do you own this vehicle?
- What adjectives describe this vehicle (old, fast, slow, sleek, big, etc.)?
- Comparing the vehicle to myself, what can I learn?

CHAPTER TWENTY-THREE

Dreams of Elevators

The first passenger elevator was installed by Elisha Graves Otis in New York in 1857—and probably not long after, people started dreaming about them.

Originally, elevators were referred to as cars and were operated by a uniformed operator. The elevator in your dream may be one of the old variety or a modern version, and these details may have some significance.

Many fear being trapped in an elevator, and any personal fear or experience with elevators should be considered when interpreting an elevator dream. Moving up in an elevator in a dream may also be symbolic of moving up in life or career, since going to a higher floor is associated with increasing awareness or status. Moving down may be losing status or esteem.

ELEVATOR NIGHTMARES

I have a couple of recurring nightmares. In one, I'm in an elevator and it won't stop at the floor I need to go to. In the other, I'm in the elevator when suddenly the cable snaps and the elevator goes crashing to the bottom.

Life may be passing this dreamer by, since the elevator won't stop on the floor she wants. She could be frustrated at not being in the right place at the right time, hence missing out on an opportunity. The second dream reflects a fear of failure caused by something beyond human control. Crashing to the bottom may indicate an inner fear that the floor will fall out of her goals, relationships, or investments. She could imagine the dream while awake and choose to take the stairs instead. This will give her back the control she seeks. If she tends to go along for the ride in life, waiting for circumstances to come her way, she could try a more assertive approach, starting with a small matter, fix her intention, and following through.

MORE ELEVATOR TERRORS

My recurring dream theme is about going up in an elevator. One was very rickety and the door kept swinging open. In another, the floor dropped as I ascended and I had to hold onto a bar across my waist. In a third version, my elevator ascended unattached from the building as if lost in space.

Elevator dreams often refer to our rise and fall in status, financial security, and awareness—big areas of life that can be influenced by outside events. This dreamer may fear that her company will not lead her to success, since the elevator is rickety, the floor falls out, or the entire car zooms into space. The good news for the dreamer is that she is always going up! Meaning she is increasing in status, awareness, or whatever applies to her life. She apparently is doing this independent of the shaky vehicle or company of which she is currently a part.

In the case of the rickety elevator in the first version of the dream, it could be that the company where she works is shaky, or at least her position in it does not feel secure. Rumors of downsizing or a merger could inspire this dream. The floor dropping out in the second version sends the message that even if the security or foundation disappears altogether, the dreamer will be safe, since there is a safety bar for her to hold onto. This again could be triggered by a company in financial difficulty, but apparently this one has a good severance package! In the third dream of space travel by elevator, the sky is the limit! Since the car is ascending, she continues to move up in status, title, or salary. This dreamer could be considering self-employment or starting her own company. Since the elevator car leaves the building, it may be that her career will zoom upward once she does leave the company she is employed by. However, she may have fears of moving up so fast, since she describes the elevator as "lost in space." This may indicate reservations about becoming isolated from others as she moves up in her career, and could explain why the dream is so uncomfortable. Working through these feelings should help.

✳

THE CASE OF THE HORIZONTAL ELEVATOR

I have never been particularly afraid of elevators but, one day at work, I was trapped in one on the way to a meeting. When no one could get the doors to open, we muscled the doors apart a few inches and realized that we were trapped between floors. It was kind of eerie. Finally, we were able to break something that allowed us to pry the doors open enough to squeeze out, but we still had to jump up to the floor, which was above our waists. The entire ordeal took about forty-five minutes. Needless to say, I was late for the meeting.

About a week later I had the following dream. I needed to get down to the third floor of a hotel; I was on an upper floor. I pushed the button to call the elevator and nothing happened. I pushed again and this time the doors did open. I got in and the doors closed, but it wouldn't budge. Finally, on the third try, the elevator car began to move down, but it wouldn't stop at the third floor, it just kept moving. When it got to the

bottom it began moving sideways. I could see out of a glass door that now
appeared, and knew that I was moving in the wrong direction, away from
where I needed to be. When the doors opened, I had only five minutes to
get to an important meeting and there was no way I could make it in
time.

At the time of this dream, the dreamer was ending one job and had
been offered another within the same company. The new position
was a lateral move. Although the security of having a new job to go
to was attractive to him, certainly better than not having a job at
all, and he was considering taking the offer, he realized that it
would require that he put on hold his desire to develop a different
career. Besides, this new position would offer nothing new to learn,
no real challenge or growth potential.

He felt that, in some ways, the new job would be a step down,
which is a reference to the elevator needing to go down and seem-
ing reluctant to move. The horizontal path of the elevator car depicts the lateral move—title and salary—and the wrong direction,
away from his own goals. Since the dreamer did not have a real-life
fear of elevators, his actual experience with the stuck elevator a
week earlier probably gave his subconscious a frame of reference to
use as a symbol. He did not want to become stuck in his career or
life.

Each new life experience becomes a potential symbol and will
represent whatever you associate with it. In this way, it is like
adding new colors of paint to your unconscious mind's palette.

The dreamer did not accept the new job offer. His dream made it
clear that this was the wrong direction and would not be satisfying.
He has decided to take the risk of changing careers and, so far, has
received a great deal of encouragement from those who can help
him. One thing to remember when taking a risk such as this is that
if you make a choice or take some action based on your own belief
in yourself, and you put everything you have into it, you won't be
sorry no matter what the outcome. If it ends up that you don't get
the results you wanted, at the very least you will know that you
tried your best and you won't sit around in old age thinking how

you wish you had just given it a try! Regrets can be very destructive and can populate our dreams with unsettling images.

A S K Y O U R S E L F

If you dream of elevators, ask yourself these questions.

- In what area of my life am I moving up or down?
- What am I concerned about losing?
- What are my current goals, what am I moving toward achieving?
- How can I insure that I don't slide backward?
- Do I fear success or failure?

CHAPTER TWENTY-FOUR

Dreams of Oceans, Lakes, Rivers, and Pools

The human body is mostly water. The seas and oceans of the earth are teeming with life. Water cleanses, and water manifests our deepest emotions in the form of tears. In the language of dreams, water is associated with God the creator as the source of all things. It is also symbolic of the unconscious mind, which can direct our lives and motivate our behavior. Dreams are one of the few ways we have of connecting with the unconscious mind, along with meditation, prayer, and art.

Water can also represent the emotional aspects of ourselves. A large body of water then would suggest deep or big emotions, choppy waters might indicate turbulent emotions, and murky water could mean that your emotions are not clear. A tidal wave is a powerful emotional upheaval. The tides come in and they go back out, the waves go up and down and, in dreams, these refer to emotional fluctuations. Animals that live in the water can be messengers from your unconscious or your emotions, bringing them into awareness.

Water and its symbolic meanings can take many forms in dreams. The presence of rain suggests emotional cleansing, and can also refer to new growth. A big storm might point toward a more turbulent emotional upset, but storms rarely last for long. A waterfall could refer to a watershed of emotion but could also evoke a beautiful and restful vacation location, or it could represent sexual release. A pool, lake, or other smaller bodies of water may represent contained emotion, things being held in. If you dream of drinking a glass of water, you may simply need to drink more water, or you may need to take in your feelings and understand them.

Naturally, as with all dream symbols, your own personal experience and associations to any water symbol will be significant in understanding your dreams.

BREATHING UNDER WATER

I am swimming in the ocean under water, but the water is clear, even clearer than a swimming pool. I am holding my breath, but realize I can no longer hold it and that my lungs are about to burst. I suddenly take a breath and realize to my extreme excitement that I can breathe under water. I swim around in awe of this. Sometimes, a dolphin swims up to me. I know it wants me to grab on to it, so I do. We swim under the water at unbelievable speeds, me breathing the whole time. When I awake, I feel great and the feeling lasts for days.

In the language of dreams, water often represents our emotional life, the feelings we have under the surface, while the solid ground represents what we knowingly communicate to others. So, these underwater dreams suggest that the dreamer is immersed in emotion. Since he can breath under water, he is comfortable with his emotional life and feelings. Since dolphins live in the water and can jump into the air, they can be messengers of our emotions—in other words they can make us aware of how we actually feel. Dolphins are associated with higher intelligence. The fact that they invite the dreamer to swim along indicates another level of comfort with his feelings. My guess is that, at times, this dreamer is uncomfortable with his feelings, he wonders if his feelings will be reciprocated, and if he is ready to take a leap and express his feelings to another person. This wonderful dream suggests that he should go ahead and jump in. Not only can he swim and survive, he can speed things up. If he does, he can experience things he never thought possible.

DREAMS OF DROWNING

Since a very young age, I have dreamed of drowning in the ocean. In my dream I begin by either wading in the ocean, sunbathing on the beach, or standing on the cliffs overlooking the ocean. Once in the water, the waves begin to get larger and larger until I am in way over my head. When I am on the shore, I'm dragged into the ocean while trying desperately to stay above the waves and not drown. I always wake up shaken by these images.

Fear of drowning in the language of dreams is a fear of getting too involved in feelings, a fear of losing one's self. As we discussed, the ocean is symbolic of our emotions and of the unconscious mind. Wading in the ocean involves flirting with emotional involvement. This dreamer is holding back, protecting her heart, not completely jumping in. Since most of her body is out of the water, she is still in control. Sunbathing on the beach is even less involved—it's like going to a party full of interesting, attractive people and choosing not to connect with anyone. Being on the cliff is somewhat dangerous, but even farther away from involvement. It's like reading the personals in the newspaper, but not following up, or making a date and then canceling it out of fear. So, this dream indicates that she considers deep feelings scary. She may have difficulty trusting and sharing her emotions. She could be avoiding relationships in order to feel in control, afraid that she could lose herself if she gets too involved. Others may find her emotionally unavailable. She may have experienced a painful loss early in life that has caused her to protect her heart.

My advice would be for the dreamer to take a good look at her relationships with those close to her, see if there are ways of becoming more intimate, sharing more of her feelings with them. She may get hurt; sometimes we are rejected, but the joy of closeness is well worth a few painful experiences.

*

SHARKS BELOW THE SURFACE

This is a recurring dream. I am beside a large body of water, either a lake or the ocean. There is a peaceful and calm tone. I am with friends, and we are enjoying our time together. Soon after, the scene changes. Clouds roll in and a storm begins. The water gets very turbulent and dark, and large waves start rolling about. Somehow, I wind up in the middle of the storm on the water. I am very afraid. I just know something under the water, like a shark or whale, is going to come up and out.

This dream indicates that learning to accept the rough waters in life, as well as the smooth sailing, can go a long way toward relieving our stress and anxiety. The recurring nature of the dream suggests a history of being at the center of conflict within a circle of friends. The relationships begin peacefully and calmly, but water often symbolizes emotion and here things really get agitated. There is a lack of truth or clarity, as symbolized by the dark color the water turns. The dreamer doesn't like the feelings she experiences in the emotional center of turbulent relationships. Her fear is based on knowing that big scary creatures can "come up and out" of her memory and hurt her again. She is on top of the water, not in the emotion, but riding on it! Is she someone who wants things to be nice and calm, who doesn't want to deal with the upsets? Does she try to make peace and shy away from conflict? Is she afraid that she will drown if she feels too deeply? Sometimes, our fear is much worse than the actual experience. Going below the surface to get in touch with any fear of getting too involved can help us recognize the source and avoid repeating past pain.

WATER, WATER, WATER

I dream of water in all forms. For example, I'm sitting on the roof of a house after a storm. There is sunshine, blue skies, nobody around—it is quiet. I am doing nothing but shooting arrows (from a bow) at turquoise paisley seahorses with very, very long eyelashes and lots of mascara.

Another dream . . . I am wandering around the courtyard of a very large home, nighttime, dim lights, wearing flowing chiffon. A fountain is spraying twenty feet into the air in the center of the courtyard. I wander, never speaking . . . looking for something. This dream recurs occasionally. I never find that someone or something.

In another dream, more like a nightmare, there are hurricane warnings. Dangerous winds are kicking up . . . rain like you have never seen—and I can't get anyone to help me board up the windows. I run around frantically boarding up windows. That's all—just boarding up windows (alone and terrified).

Another dream . . . I live in the river, dark and murky. I swim back and forth, shore to shore. I hope nobody sees me. My head is always above the water, quiet, the lights shimmering off the water. I'm careful not to go to the black part of the river, I sure don't want anyone to see me . . . I'm frightened.

Well, it goes on and on . . . suffice it to say there's just always water of some sort in my dreams. I am curious about that. Sometimes I'm terrified, sometimes I'm calm . . . most of the time I'm frustrated.

The larger lesson of all of these dreams may emerge if we understand each one, so, let's take them in order. If the seahorses in the first dream had to be someone the dreamer knows, or herself, who would they be? Who wears a lot of mascara? The emotional storm is over but she sits high above the surface and shoots arrows. Clearly she retains some anger.

In the next dream, she is in an opulent setting. A fountain represents beauty and life (the fountain of youth?). She searches for someone or something, but she is going around in circles. Perhaps the dreamer feels that she is chasing her youth.

In the next, a hurricane is approaching. In dreams, hurricanes represent a collection of turbulent emotions; they can wipe out a community. No one is there to help her protect her home. If the windows are the eyes, this dream suggests that she doesn't want to see this trouble coming, and that she feels alone in dealing with it, unprotected. The hurricane could reflect a feeling that if she were to actually get in touch with her feelings, the crying wouldn't stop.

In the last dream, in which she lives in the water, she is immersed in her emotions. There, she doesn't want to be seen, avoiding the dark or unknown part of her emotions. I suspect that she is alone. Fearful of being found out as emotionally vulnerable, she hides. She doesn't want to be alone, and yet she doesn't want to be hurt. By keeping her head above water, she tries to maintain mental control of the situation.

This dreamer may have had an early emotional injury, but therapy seems in order to help unravel this mystery. Once done, she may move on to have healthy and happy relationships. This dreamer clearly has some work to do in accepting her emotions and being free to love. Her dreams seem to be bringing these protective mechanisms into her awareness, so that she can get the appropriate assistance.

NUDE SWIMMER

I had a very odd dream the other night. I went on a family vacation (although I don't recall seeing my family members, I just felt their presence). We went to a country inn with plaster walls and exposed beams—just like an early seventeenth century home. It must have been late spring or early summer, because the sun was very bright and warm. Alongside my room (bottom floor) was a cool and shaded deck that looked out onto a large lake. The lake had crystal blue water, as clear as the Mediterranean Sea.

In the lake were swimming an assortment of miniature sea-monsterlike fishes, only these monsters were the size of a house cat or large dog, and they swam both in and atop the water, like fish or ducks. I was afraid of the monsters, but was enthralled by their existence and sheer number. There were so many of them (and so many varieties), that I could not understand how they had the space to move, and I could barely see the real fish, such as normal-sized bass, and the like.

Off to the side was a young woman, whom I thought rather over-weight and plain when I saw her walking around the inn. (Actually, she looked a lot like me.) She waded into the water stark naked, but appeared very beautiful this time. I had been afraid to go into the water in case some venomous creature might sting me, but I was left with a serene feeling nevertheless, and could not let my eyes drift away from the scene at my feet.

The dreamer is the woman that she observes, and the sea monsters are family members with whom she fears getting into emotional waters. In dreams, monsters represent the ugly, repressed feelings haunting the dreamer. These live inside us but can surface as well; we can't really escape them.

The number of monsters may refer to the size of her family, or to all of the dark and difficult emotions she feels where they are concerned. Once she goes into the water, and is willing to feel her feelings and interact with her family, she emerges beautiful and serene. Nudity in a dream can mean that others will not reject you when you express your true self.

This dreamer should let herself swim and take a dive into her feelings—it won't be as bad as she fears, and the results will be wonderful.

ASK YOURSELF

If you have dreams of water, ask yourself these questions.

- What are my true feelings at this time?
- What do I fear?
- What would make me more comfortable with my relationships?
- Do I need to cleanse any old messages out of my consciousness?
- How can I be more comfortable being me?

Dreams of Disaster

Disaster dreams include plane crashes, earthquakes, tornadoes, and tidal waves. These dreams often occur when we are going through major changes, either positive or negative. Getting fired, finding out you are pregnant, even a move could inspire such a dream. (Some people do actually dream of a disaster before one does occur. While this is rare, it is a good idea to prepare, just in case.) Changes bring with them the opportunity for growth and new beginnings. Even though the dream may seem very dramatic, the actual cause is most often an emotional upheaval.

As with all dreams, if your actual life experience reflects the elements in your dreams, consider your personal memories and associations before analyzing any symbolic meaning. I have lived through a few major earthquakes, one causing extensive damage to my home and a huge disruption in my life. Even after I moved to an area on the East Coast not at all known for earthquakes, I would brace myself when I felt a rumbling. Usually it was something as benign as a bus going over a pothole, but it brought the same instant sense of panic to me. Likewise, any disaster we have lived through can seep back into our lives through our dreams; you may be processing feelings about the disaster. Nightmares and recurring disaster dreams can be a symptomatic of post-traumatic stress disorder (PTSD). Other symptoms may mimic depression or anxiety and include an obsession with the news or other media depicting the situation that caused the stress. If you believe you may be experiencing post-traumatic stress disorder, discuss your symptoms with your physician. This is an area of medicine that in recent years has become better understood, and good help is available.

The disaster may also be a personal symbol, your own private shorthand for what you actually felt at the time. So, in my case, an earthquake could represent a giant disruption, being displaced from my home, or losing my material possessions.

※

TORNADOES

I have a recurring dream in which I am being chased by tornadoes. In one, I am running down the street in my hometown in England, being chased by tornadoes. I duck into a church to get away. In another, I run through a field as tornadoes touch down all around me. They never seem to hurt me but I wake up feeling threatened.

Waking up with a residual feeling of being threatened is a sign to ask yourself, "What risk am I in at this time? How can I protect myself?" In the language of dreams, tornadoes represent turmoil, conflict, fighting, danger, and feeling out of control—in other words, a major upset. Any dream that depicts a childhood home can represent issues that were dealt with at that time, or an old pattern repeating itself. Was this dreamer's childhood one of conflict and unpredictability? Is he feeling as vulnerable as a child might at the present time? Church often represents a safe place or neutral zone. It could be that he prayed for protection as a child.

In the second version of the dream, he runs through an open

field, the tornadoes or conflicts all around, but never actually touching him. Tornadoes are fast-moving air—air being symbolic of consciousness, intellect, and thought. So, it would seem that the upset is more mental or verbal than physical. Is he a major worrier? Is he surrounded by argumentative people? They don't pick on him, but he is still unsettled by their proximity. He should avoid these high-drama people and situations if possible, not letting them suck him into their conflicts. If the destructive thoughts are his own, he can seek to understand why he has them. Worrying won't help. Create a plan and take action.

GIANT WAVES

I have a recurring dream in which I am in a little house floating in the ocean. I am with my three children. We can see the shoreline through the front windows. We appear to be relaxed and having a good time.

When I turn to face the open sea, I can see a woman (it could be me, but I cannot see her face) looking out the back window toward the ocean.

There is a gigantic wave approaching. I am petrified. I yell for the woman to get away from the window, but she doesn't move. She doesn't seem afraid. The huge wave is roaring toward the little house. I scramble to get my kids. I don't know how I can carry them all to shore. The wave crashes into the house and rolls it over and over. To my surprise, the window that the woman was standing in front of does not break and no water seeps into the house.

I wish my boyfriend could help me, but someone says he is sick. In the end, he appears in the water and helps me bring the children to safety.

The little house in this dream represents the dreamer, as does the woman at the window. She feels safe and content, then the gigantic wave approaches. The wave could represent a major, unexpected emotional confrontation. The good news is that she survives. If she sometimes doubts that her boyfriend will be there to help her with the children, it appears from this dream that she can count on him.

A single mother will often have anxiety dreams. Concern for

her ability to be everywhere at once when her children need her is terrifying. This dreamer seems to be reassured by her dream, that she does have help and, even in the face of danger, all will endure.

A s k   Y o u r s e l f

If you have disaster dreams, ask yourself the following questions.

- Have I actually experienced a disaster? Am I still fearful?
- What is upsetting me at this time? Am I anticipating a major upset?
- What can I do to be prepared for the unexpected?
- What emotional or mental feeling could make me feel exposed to danger?
- Who can I talk with to feel reassured?

CHAPTER TWENTY-SIX

Dreams of Blood and Violence

We are inundated by violent images these days. Movies, television, music videos, and even the nightly news display shootings and other violent acts. So, there is a concrete frame of reference for violent dreams. If you have been the actual victim of a crime, then your dream could be a symptom of post-traumatic stress. You may be reliving the crime as a way of healing or your subconscious mind may be suggesting that you reach out for help. In that case, therapy can be very helpful, as can writing in a journal, as well as self-defense classes, to increase self-confidence and a sense of personal empowerment.

Blood, of course, is necessary for life and, in dreams, it represents life force and life energy. If you are bleeding, you are losing your life force. Who is causing you to do this? Are you bleeding yourself of energy by letting intrusive thoughts rob your energy? If you receive a transfusion in a dream, who is the source of new life or energy? If blood is on your hands, you may feel guilty about something you have caused or participated in. A vampire sucking your blood can represent a person or circumstance that is robbing you of energy.

Violence in dreams can be a reflection of anger if you are the perpetrator, or vulnerability if you are the victim. It can also reflect a balancing act. If you have an overbearing and unreasonable boss, spouse, or neighbor, for example, you may dream of shooting or stabbing him or her! This can be very disturbing, but it may just be a stress-management technique that, on a certain level, helps disperse resentment and level the playing field. It can also reveal the anger you may have repressed and are unaware of in your waking state, so that you can make an effort to communicate or repair a situation. Of course, you would never act on the images in any of these dreams; they are simply your very private venting method.

SHOT BY POLICE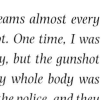

I am a twenty-year-old woman, and I have these dreams almost every night. I am being chased. I always end up getting shot. One time, I was hit by thirty rounds, and then turned into an old lady, but the gunshot wounds did not hurt. I never died; it just felt like my whole body was asleep. Another time, I was in my car being chased by the police, and they ended up unloading multiple rounds, but only one bullet hit me in the neck. Again, I did not die—the wound did not even hurt. There was just a lot of blood.

Being chased in a dream involves being pursued by something. The person chasing us can symbolize a deadline, an addiction, or an actual bully about whom we have a real concern.

Ruling out a concrete basis for violent dreams, we can reflect on these dreams as symbols and metaphor. Bullets, in the language of dreams, are something that penetrates our body. They are shot from a gun, which can be a symbol of protection or aggression. In the first dream, this young woman is hit by "thirty rounds" and she turns into an old lady. I would ask her if the number thirty is significant to her. Guns can also be viewed as symbols of aggressive male sexuality. I wonder if she has a boyfriend and if she feels pressure to have sex with him. Turning into an old lady may make her less sexually desirable and, perhaps, safer from this aggression. Of course, turning into an old lady means that she did survive the shooting. Her body feeling asleep or numb could also refer to how she deals with unwanted sexual advances. Some women learn to split off from or not even feel their bodies when they are having sex.

In the second dream, the police are chasing the dreamer. Police represent authority figures, their purpose to serve and protect. Of course they may be corrupt or trigger-happy, too. In this dream, they managed to hit her in the neck. The neck is the outside covering of the throat, which is often associated with communication. "Sticking your neck out" is taking a risk and "necking" is a passionate kissing session. Does she feel that she can't trust the authority figures in her life to protect her? Or that she doesn't have the authority or power to stop an aggressive act directed at her? She is losing blood and life force over this issue. I would suggest that she play detective and figure out what is the cause of this distress, and remedy the situation before it totally drains her.

This could be the dream of a woman who has a boyfriend and is afraid to tell him that she doesn't want to have sex with him for fear of losing him. Metaphorically, she may subject herself to bullets (penetration) and even split off or go numb in the process. We must feel free to communicate our truth to have the life we want. You may fool yourself or your boyfriend, but you cannot fool your subconscious mind, and the truth will all come out in your dreams.

✳

BANK ROBBERS

I once had a dream that I was in a bank witnessing a robbery. In the dream, I am only seven years old. Fearing for my life, I try to escape, but am caught. I break down and begin to cry. The robber grabs hold of my shirt and brings his gun to my head. He pulls the trigger and instantly I wake with a splitting headache. This is the only time I ever woke abruptly from a dream.

It is likely that this dreamer had the headache first, and that his subconscious wove the pain into his dream. This can happen when our bodies are experiencing any stimuli and we are in the dream state. The dream does, of course, have meaning as well. He is an innocent caught in a situation of someone else's doing. Something of value is being taken and he can't escape being caught in the danger. He can ask himself where this fits into his life, and he will have the explanation of the dream. An example would be if he were part of a management team, and the team leader fired someone that he felt was doing a fine job. The team members have to present a united front but, since he feels the person didn't deserve to be fired, that makes him feel guilty. He doesn't want to be blamed, and he doesn't want the person to look to him and feel betrayed.

SCHOOL SHOOTINGS

I often have dreams of wartime scenarios or combat situations in a variety of settings. Sometimes, I will be in high school and all of a sudden the scene will turn into a surprise guerrilla attack. Many times, I will be engaged in armed conflict, and the bullets in my rifle will fall and no damage will be inflicted on the target. Or, I might pick up a rifle that had been functioning perfectly and now won't shoot.

Life can feel like a battle when we are involved in conflicts, either internal (such as trying to overcome a bad habit or control anger) or external (in conflict with others). It would seem that this dreamer feels attacked, and doesn't always have the ammunition he needs to fight back. This could be a matter of not being able to say what he wants when he wants to. Many people experience this when they are verbally attacked; it is only after the other person walks away that they find the right response. This can be maddening! There are a couple of things a person in this situation might try. First, practice: get a friend and role-play some situations in which you have been ineffective as a communicator. Take your time. Play both roles—yourself, and the other person. Practice saying just the right thing to resolve the conflict. It is almost always best to take the high road and be the bigger person. Still, there are ways to put a difficult or critical person in his or her place or set the record straight.

If this is not enough, there are classes in communication skills available at community colleges and through other organizations—they can be very helpful. It is fun to get some tools and practice under your belt, so that you will be ready the next time and won't have to feel that your mouth is misfiring!

MURDERED HER SISTER

My sister and I are both in the midst of painful crises. As children, we were bitter rivals, mostly because we were opposites in many ways. With maturity, we realize that we were both jealous of the other's qualities. We are close now. We still don't share a deep emotional bond, but we are affectionate and loving.

In the past few years, I have dreamed several times that I murdered my sister. In each dream, the method is different but the reasoning is the same. I have a bizarre compulsion to kill my sister in order to prevent her from knowing heartache. In one dream, I drowned her in a bathtub so that she wouldn't know she had given birth to a dead baby. In all of these dreams, I am screaming in pain. My screaming and crying wake me up and I discover that I have been crying for some time. My face is soaked and my throat is raw.

In a woman's dream, a sister is often an aspect of the dreamer herself. In other words, she represents the part of the woman that could be described by the same adjectives we would use to describe her. This dreamer says that she and her sister are opposites in many ways; it would seem then that they are mirrors and teachers to one another in important ways. Maybe this woman really feels as though part of her is dying. Maybe she wants to annihilate her own pain. If there are still residual feelings of jealousy, then the dream may refer back to Cain and Abel or back to ancient mythical stories. Perhaps it is easier to focus on what the sister is going through than to think about her own difficulties.

This dreamer is not her sister's keeper. None of us can be spared the lessons we need to learn—adversity makes us who we are, strengthening and defining us. Being available to listen, hold a hand, or just be with a sister or friend is the best way to help. Asking her directly, "What can I do?" is also a wonderful way to support her. The dreamer should do the same for herself, too. Maybe she can take time out for a massage or a walk in the park or around the block. She should nurture herself and know that love does not mean protecting someone from living or making their own choices. If we anticipate the needs of others and cushioned every fall, they will never learn how to pick themselves up and start over.

The details of the dream are powerfully suggestive. A baby in a dream can represent a new creative project, a bathtub can stand for cleansing, and drowning suggests being overwhelmed with emotion—suffocated by it. Perhaps this woman has recently given up on an idea or project that was very dear to her. A new business failing would be an example. To avoid the humiliation, she might want to just hide or go away. If something like this happened to the sister, perhaps this dreamer is just being very empathetic toward her loss. Either way, dying is never the answer. When we face our choices, bad and good, we learn, grow, mature and become more effective, efficient, and joyful.

ASK YOURSELF

If you dream of blood or violence ask yourself these questions.

- Am I losing energy, depressed, or fatigued?
- Can I isolate the cause of this depletion?
- What changes can I make to balance the stress in my life?
- Am I angry with myself or with anyone else?
- How can I resolve these feelings?

CHAPTER TWENTY-SEVEN

Dreams of Animals

When animals appear in dreams, we are often being reminded of our primitive or instinctual natures. The qualities of the animal are significant, as are our own associations and any actual life experience with the animal. Ask yourself what comes to mind when you think of this animal. If you have a history with the animal or type of animal, bring those experiences to mind and jot down your memories in your dream journal.

If you dream of animals, write four or five descriptive words that come to mind when you think of the animal; these will be your best clues as to what the animal means to you symbolically. If you feel that the meaning is more complex, you might benefit from reading a bit about the characteristics of the animal. Use an encyclopedia, dictionary, the Internet, or the library. What are its unique characteristics? What is it known for?

Animal folklore can also reveal important associations. Although the ostrich doesn't actually bury its head in the sand, it is known for that behavior. Therefore, a dream of an ostrich could symbolize not wanting to see something. Ignorance may not be bliss. If you dream of an ostrich, avoiding the truth may get you into trouble and your dream may be trying to give you a heads up. A turtle or a tortoise in your dream may refer to the famous fable "The Tortoise and the Hare," in which the tortoise, the slower of the two animals, wins the race through perseverance. Therefore, the tortoise in your dream may represent sticking to your goal and not giving up.

When trying to understand the meaning of the animal, also consider if the animal in your dream is realistic in appearance or is a cartoon depiction. What is the animal doing? Is its behavior normal for this creature?

All of the details can help reveal the meaning of the animals in your dreams. Once you establish that, say, chickens mean cowardice to you, your subconscious mind will use that symbol again when you need to get that message. Keeping your own symbol guide will become an invaluable resource. Domestic animals have different meanings than those residing in the desert, jungle, or forest. The desert is sparse, its creatures survive well in heat, the jungle offers tropical and exotic images, and the forest may bring to mind lush and magical images. Sometimes, the animals in dreams can talk or communicate telepathically. Pay particular attention to any quality or ability that the animal does not possess in its actual existence. Note how you feel about the specific animal in your dream. Is it warm and friendly or threatening, for example?

✳

A DOCTOR'S DREAM

I am a physician. I am frustrated with my lifestyle. I enjoy work, but want more leisure time. In my dream, I caught three successively larger fish, the last one unusual and huge. During the dream, my husband helped me get the barb of a fishhook out of my finger, and my dad (who is deceased) ignored my request for help. The first fish was distinctive and colorful and I wanted my dad to hit it on the head to kill it.

Since, in the language of dreams, water represents the unconscious mind and our emotions, this dream indicates that a woman is searching her mind deeply for answers. The act of fishing symbolizes a search for nourishment of the spirit, the place this dreamer's frustration and unrest dwell. Since she catches fish, she is pulling up messages from the unconscious. However, fishing is also a great leisure activity, a way to unwind and play, and that is what this dream is exploring. Although the first fish is "distinctive and colorful," or interesting, she wants it dead! Thus, a part of her may be fighting this change of lifestyle. There is a certain comfort in routine, even if it is somewhat boring. Since the father ignores her request for help, I suspect that he wasn't always a good listener or supportive of her desires. Perhaps he saw work as worthwhile and leisure as a waste of time. The husband, on the other hand, is there to support her when the dreamer gets a little hurt or things don't go exactly as planned.

The number three is significant, for it represents the balance of body, mind, and spirit. Since the three fish get larger as the dreamer continues, it seems that she is testing the idea of living more leisurely a little at a time, increasing slowly. I would suggest that she choose a leisure activity that she can fit into her schedule, release the ghost of her father and his definition of a good life, and try to restore balance to her life. The colorful and unusual characteristics of the fish indicate that she would like to do something a little exciting.

Fish in this dream are messengers from the dreamer's unconscious mind. The biblical story of feeding the multitudes with a few fishes also comes to mind and may represent the spiritual sustenance for which the dreamer longs.

DEVOTED TO HER DOG

I am walking down a rather ugly street in Hollywood. I am barefoot—in fact, all I am wearing is a towel! I am embarrassed by my nudity, but even more so because my hair is only towel-dried and is still quite damp. It looks like a tangled haystack. I keep one hand on the towel and, with the other, I try to cover my face and head. I go into a souvenir store and get a shirt, but nothing for my hair because people start to point at me and I have to leave. I see my car parked under an apartment building, I start to get in it, but then I see my little dog running down the street looking for me, so I go back outside to get him. I am still embarrassed because people are staring at me.

Dreams are often quite unrealistic. If she actually did walk the streets of Hollywood in nothing but a towel, it might not even generate a raised eyebrow! But this dreamer is clearly feeling vulnerable and out of place. Hollywood is associated with show business and glamor, but also with illusion and facade. The "rather ugly" part of Hollywood that she finds herself in is certainly an undesirable place to be alone and in need. She is very concerned about how she looks, and doesn't like the attention she receives. Yet, she is not so vain that her discomfort keeps her from rescuing her pet. In real life, as in Hollywood, appearances can be deceiving; hair, make-up, and wardrobe can change a person's look completely, and disguise a true or false intent. In this dream, the self reveals its true colors— risking embarrassment to save her little dog. The dreamer may feel valued more for her appearance than for her heart and compassion. Here, rescuing her "little dog" was her subconscious mind's way of demonstrating what is truly important in life. Her devotion to her pet overrode all other feelings of personal discomfort.

TIPPI HEDREN'S DREAM

Boomer, my handsome, big-guy lion was at the airport getting ready to board our plane to London, when I saw that he was standing on his hind legs and was dressed like a gentleman in a bowler hat, camel-hair coat, with a cane over his shoulder. We walked arm in arm. Boomer looked at me but nobody else paid any attention to this amazing scene.

Famed for her roles in such Alfred Hitchcock films as *The Birds* and as mother of Melanie Griffith, Hedren founded and runs the Shambala Animal Preserve in Acton, California. She rescues unwanted, injured, and aging wild animals, and restores them to health. In the language of dreams, lions represent power and strength. They are kings of the jungle and Boomer is certainly dressed regally here! Through Tippi's association with animals, she also feels powerful and strong. Beyond that, obviously, she is friends with her favorite pets. Her dream shows that she considers them equal in importance to humans. Being out in the world with her lion, she reveals her desire that the world accept animals and their needs as she does.

ASK YOURSELF

- What are my first thoughts about this animal?
- Do I have any personal experience with this type of animal?
- What are the natural characteristics of this animal?
- What unrealistic characteristics or qualities did the animal in my dream present?
- In what ways am I similar to or different from this animal?

Dreams of Birds and Bugs

Birds and all manner of insects seem to populate the dreams of many people. Each of these creatures has universal meanings, as well as personal ones. If you have a fear of any living thing and dream of it, it may simply represent fear. If you had a pet parakeet as a child and dream of little Tweety, your dream may take you back to that time in your life and how you felt about your pet. Horror movies are also filled with these creatures, and they can make our nocturnal dramas pretty creepy.

In general, birds represent freedom. A caged bird, then, represents being, or at least feeling, trapped. *Birdbrain* is slang for someone who does stupid things, and *jailbird* is the colloquial term for someone just out of prison. More specifically, the eagle, king of all fowl, soars above the earth and has a high perch, a vantage point from which to observe. It can focus on the tiniest details. Eagles can also represent distinction. A penguin can't fly and lives in a frozen climate. It can represent stiff formality. Black and white in color, it can also embody good and evil in one being. The male peacock is known for showing off to attract the opposite sex. In a dream, it may represent boasting or pride. *Turkey* is slang for a dud, something that just didn't turn out right. This may be because the poor bird has a terrible time trying to fly, and it has become dinner to many Americans every Thanksgiving.

Bugs in general represent an annoyance—something is bugging you. Some are associated with filth, and many people have some degree of fear of at least one type of insect. Ask yourself, what is bothering me? (If you have a serious allergy to a specific insect's sting or bite, you must take this into consideration when interpreting your dream.) Spiders are associated with the gods, who weave the web of human destiny. Are you trying to catch or manipulate someone or something? If you fear these leggy creatures, they may represent another unrelated fear in your dream, possibly offering a method of understanding or overcoming it. A snail—not an insect, but still a pest—is smart enough to carry its home with it, but it moves so slowly. Are you taking a snail's pace in your life? Ants are considered industrious and well-organized, but they also can ruin a picnic. Tiny things, they can build huge anthills and carry items larger than they are. Look to the nature and characteristics of any creature for hints as to what it represents in your dream.

FEATHERED FRIENDS

I dreamed that little birds of various sizes and colors were getting into our house. They had managed to peck holes in the screens, and even the floor, so that they could get inside. There were so many birds that I was getting panicky about how I would get them out of the house. I got very upset when I noticed that the birds, especially the smallest ones, were falling to the floor and dying. I opened all the doors and windows, and was very relieved to watch them all fly out, even the ones that had fallen.

Ever feel as though ideas are just flying around in your head? This dreamer's peace of mind had gone to the birds—birds in this case representing intruding thoughts. Air is often symbolic of intellect, ideas, and communication. Since birds live and fly in the air, they can be messengers of these thoughts and ideas. Perhaps this dream is about being exposed to many ideas and opinions, about too much input. Bombarded with her own thoughts and other people's ideas, the dreamer can't think for herself and feels confused. Some ideas are dying before she even gets to consider them. Since the birds are even coming in through the floor, the dream suggests that her very foundation has holes in it. When she opens the windows and doors, she opens her mind as well, releasing the ideas and thoughts. A house can be symbolic for our bodies, the doors open or close our hearts, all the windows may represent our eyes or what we are willing to look at. The relief she feels when the birds all fly away suggests that she needs to remain open, not seeking or accepting too much advice at one time, for it can confuse her. The dreamer can gain clarity by pushing unsolicited ideas out of her mind.

DREAM OF BEES

For many years, I have had the same dream in which bees are trying to get into my ear. I am always surrounded by ten or twenty of them and they are trying to get into my ear. I can both see and hear them very vividly. The last time, the bee was a huge bumblebee of two to three inches in diameter. It was trying to get into my ear and the sound stayed in my mind for days.

Bees are organized, hard workers. They also cause fear in many. These insects represent contrast, since they make sweet honey and they also sting. Life requires us to take the bitter with the sweet— cold days of winter help us appreciate the hot days of summer. Indeed, few things in life are all bad or all good. Ruling out a fear of bees or an actual buzzing in the dreamer's ear caused by a physical problem (such as the side effect of a prescription medication), this dream may indicate a need to accept the good with the bad.

The dreamer could also have this dream when she is as busy as a bee and needs to add some balance and relaxation to her life. Always rule out the obvious first before looking to your dream as symbolic.

*

BUGGED BY BUGS

My frequent dream is that I am on my adult children's patio. I see bugs all over and try to sweep them under the rug. I can never get all of them and I awake feeling really frustrated.

Bugs can represent little annoyances or big things that are really bugging us. Since, in this dream, the man is at the home of his adult children, I can take a guess and assume that there are things they do that bug him. Maybe they just do things differently than he would. Maybe he fears that their choices will lead to trouble down the road. In either case, apparently, he doesn't feel comfortable expressing his views. Since this dream is recurring, he may want to initiate a conversation. Perhaps he could take a walk with one of his children and discuss any concerns he has in a nonassertive manner. Simply talking about how things were different from the way he was taught or believes is appropriate and may solve the problem. He may be surprised; his children may appreciate hearing his opinions. Either way, he will have spoken his piece and the dream will probably stop occurring.

It can be so hard to stand silently by and watch others make choices or behave in ways we feel are just wrong. Learning to share a thought or opinion without becoming the ultimate authority or becoming too persuasive or manipulative is an art worth learning.

SPIDERS IN THE BED

In my dream, I am lying in bed when suddenly there are black spiders all over my sheets and pillows. They start to crawl on my body. I get so frightened that I throw off the covers and jump out of bed. Then, I wake up and find that I actually have jumped out of bed and am standing there searching for spiders. The funny thing is that, in real life, I am not afraid of spiders or bugs.

I once had a similar dream, and there actually was a spider in my bed. This type of dream could be generated by something that really is making you itch, an allergy to a fabric or the detergent used on your sheets, for example. If that is not the case, spiders in dreams can indicate that something is pestering you. A spider spins a sticky trap of manipulation. Dreaming of spiders may mean that the dreamer is uncomfortable with the real-life web she has created, even though she has probably created it unconsciously. The spiders are black, which is symbolic of the unknown. She should take an honest look at the controls, conditions, and rules she applies to others in her life. Does she really want all those little flies she's attracted into her web? She may feel that it is the opposite, that she is caught in someone else's web of control. If so, she should try to determine who and what has her caught, and take measures to exit as soon as possible.

It is interesting that this dreamer does not have a fear of insects in her waking life. Clearly, then, the spiders reflect something truly disturbing to her. The nature of the spider is the key to understanding this dream. Only the dreamer knows if she is the web spinner or the innocent one caught in the web.

ASK YOURSELF

If you have dreams of birds or bugs, ask yourself these questions.

- Is anything bugging me that I have not expressed toward those involved?
- Are my thoughts interfering with my productivity?
- What are the particular characteristics of the creatures in my dream?
- Is my life affected by those same characteristics?
- Do I have any fear of the creature in my dream; am I facing a fear at this time?

Dreams of School and Tests

Dreams of being back in school offer a lesson or learning opportunity, so pay attention to what is being taught. If an Asian teacher appears in your dream, for example, your unconscious may be indicating that something from Eastern philosophy would benefit you. If you dream about being back in the school you actually attended, you may be dealing with issues or lessons from that time that have come back into focus. Elementary school, for instance, can be a symbol of that period of your life.

The world is a classroom, and we are learning every day. Every experience offers an opportunity for growth and lessons, and these lessons will repeat in various ways until we learn them. A common dream theme is that of being at school and knowing there is a test to take. We may feel that we have not attended the class, or that we have not studied. Sometimes, we can't even find the classroom. These dreams occur when we feel that we will be judged or tested in our waking life. Going to a job-review meeting with your boss or going on a job interview can spawn this dream theme. Reinforcing your sense of self-confidence and self-worth will be helpful to combat the anxiety that comes with this dream. Make all the proper preparations and remind yourself of past successes.

COLLEGE EXAM

I am an undergraduate in a classroom at college, awaiting the administration of the final exam. I enrolled in this one, but, unlike all my other classes, never attended a class or did any of the work. I don't even know what course this is! The exam is being held in a typical classroom and some of the people look vaguely familiar but I don't know them personally.

This man describes the quintessential test and school dream. Being unprepared for an exam in a dream reflects the times in life when we have felt tested and unprepared. We fear failure, harsh judgment, and the criticism of strangers. Usually, these fears are unfounded, since we typically sail through life's tests unscathed. When we do fail at something in life, it is our opportunity to reevaluate our circumstances and gain personal insight. Sometimes more instruction is necessary, but, at other times, more personal awareness is warranted. Understanding what motivates our behavior is the big lesson because, once understood, we take control and can make the appropriate choices in our lives. In this way, we can accomplish our goals. Otherwise, we continue living unaware and may sabotage our success without realizing it.

So, since this dreamer appears as an undergraduate, he may need to realize that there is more to learn in this lifetime, but he can't move on until he has learned the lesson at hand. We can't learn algebra until we can multiply and divide. I would remind this dreamer that he does have certain skills, capabilities, and past successes, and that being open to learning each lesson along the way should alleviate the anxiety that this dream indicates.

If test taking is a frequent theme in your dreams, it can be very helpful to keep a journal and write in it something new that you have learned every single day. Reviewing this learning journal from time to time, especially just before facing a challenging situation, will go a long way toward bolstering your confidence.

✳

SCHOOL BOMB

I dreamed that I secretly planted a nuclear bomb at a school, then ran to hide in some tall grass before it exploded. As I was waiting for the blast, two elephants almost ran over me in their attempt to get away from the imminent explosion. I remember that one elephant's trunk was tied in knots in two places, and I thought in my dream that it was good luck to see an elephant with knots in its trunk!

Bombs are small things with powerful destructive potential. Perhaps this dreamer knows of someone with a temper who could be described this way. Dreams with bombs usually involve the anger of the dreamer or a fear of an explosive person.

As for the elephants, it is said that an elephant never forgets. As such, they are associated with memory. Perhaps this dreamer felt humiliated at school and wants to express her anger by blowing it up.

Elephants are also huge and relate to things of enormous size; they almost trampled the dreamer. What in her waking life might snuff her out? The trunk of the elephant is another interesting element. Ordinarily, the trunk provides the elephant's method of drinking, trumpeting, and reaching for food, and one of these has knots in his. In the language of dreams, a knot is usually a tangled mess we need to sort out. A stomach tied up in knots represents emotional stress. Knots can strengthen but, here, they would make the elephant unable to drink, reach for food, or trumpet. Yet, to the dreamer, this is a sign of luck. Was there a big person who picked on her or was loud and obnoxious to her, when she was in school?

It is also possible that school simply represents a lesson the dreamer doesn't want to learn—after all, she wants to blow the whole thing up. She should try to determine what in her life she would like to see blown away or obliterated. Is something explosive, about to break apart? What makes her angry? She should seek to understand and make repairs without taking drastic measures.

TEST AND BABY

In a recurring dream, I am back in college. A final is coming up and I haven't studied or been to class. I don't even know what period the class is or where it meets. In my second recurring dream, I suddenly remember to my horror that I have a baby and haven't fed it in a day or so.

The test theme in dreams refers to the many ways in which we feel tested in life. Whenever we are in a situation where we know our abilities and efforts will be judged, we may feel some anxiety. We want to pass the test and get a good grade. When she had this dream, she probably felt insecure and/or unprepared for something in her waking life. (I have had this dream, too, as most adults have, and it can be very frustrating.)

Not doing what we should have or neglecting our responsibilities can result in a test dream. The cause and the result of remembering the dream are the same: anxiety. Sometimes we are just trying to do too many things in our twenty-four-hour day. It can be hard to say no to new obligations when someone thinks you are capable of handling them, because the faith they have in us feels good. Remember though, it is *your* twenty-four hours, and you need at least eight of them for sleep. Time management or better organization may be the answer.

Babies can represent concepts to which we have given birth, so the second dream in which she has neglected her baby indicates that she has ignored a creative project. It appears she will fail this test, too, since not feeding the baby will surely result in its death. Neglecting our projects and goals causes them to die as well.

Both dreams indicate that she is a caring and concerned person. If the test dream continues to recur, she should take all necessary steps to prepare for whatever she is involved in. If the neglected baby dream recurs, she needs to look to any important project or endeavor in her life, and be sure it is getting the attention it deserves.

ASK YOURSELF

If you have dreams of school or tests, ask yourself these questions.

- What lesson should I be learning?
- Where in my life do I feel tested?
- How can I be better prepared?
- If I am prepared, how can I release this anxiety?
- Can I take measures to become more organized?
- What would I especially like to learn right now?

Dreams of Bathrooms

Dreams that include bathrooms are very common. Children will often dream of using the toilet while they are actually wetting the bed. They are often confused when they wake up wet, because the dream was so real that they would swear they had actually gotten up and walked into the bathroom.

Adults also have this dream when the actual call of nature arises, although we usually recognize the warning in time to wake up, thank goodness. But bathrooms, toilets, showers, and the activities that take place in this room are also powerful symbols of other things.

Toilets are where we let go of material we have processed and no longer need. We have gotten our use from the situation, we have learned what we need, and now we need to let go and move on. Showers and baths are obviously involved with cleansing, and also with preparing or getting ready. Thus, cleaning up a situation can be represented by a bath or shower. Some of these bathroom dreams include an element of shame, such as when a toilet is only available in a public place, thus adding humiliation to the releasing process.

I have had two series of toilet dreams in my own life, the first when I was a teenager. At the time I was very active in my church and spirituality was very important to me. Indeed, the only way I knew to be close to God was through the church. I was a lay reader (I would take turns with others reading the Old Testament lesson during the Sunday services), I was a Sunday-school teacher, and I was on a committee reviewing a proposal to change the language used for worship services to more modern English in a effort to attract more parishioners and make God easier to understand. (I voted against it—I like the *thees* and *thous!*)

During this time, I became disenchanted with the church. I loved it, but it didn't answer all of my questions. There was so much more that I wanted to know and a lot of the answers I received seemed pat, rehearsed, and not well thought out. I felt as though the church was discouraging me from thinking on my own about deep spiritual matters. It was as if to be a good Christian, I should just memorize and use the same answers the church elders offered.

I began having dreams in which a church minister had defecated in an old-fashioned chamber pot. I took this to mean that what he was putting out was old-fashioned and outdated—some of it may have been crap! In other words, my subconscious mind was suggesting that I take my spiritual quest elsewhere. I began to study many different religions and philosophies. I still love religion and the various churches, mosques, and temples of the world. Many provide a beautiful service for their members. I have also learned that it is all right to question. It is important to continue to seek answers to the questions that live in our souls until they are satisfied. Spiritual awareness or enlightenment is a process that lasts a lifetime.

The second series of toilet dreams came many years ago, while I was in a romantic relationship that had become emotionally abusive. The downturn in the relationship was so subtle I didn't really see it coming, but my boyfriend had become angry, demeaning, and, somewhere along the way, I lost myself.

My dreams at this time always involved needing to use a toilet and not being able to find one. Sometimes I would follow signs through a maze only to find dressing rooms but no toilet. Other times, the toilets would be filthy, or in public view, or primitive, such as a floor sink toilet, such as I had seen while traveling in third-world countries. This recurring theme was telling me to let go of the relationship. I had gotten the good out of it and it was time now to let go. I worried about how others would be affected—hence the public toilets. I was also concerned that it might get messy if I made my feelings known—which explains the often filthy conditions. I was also ashamed that I had not been more in control; how could I have let this go so long? When my boyfriend and I agreed to an amicable parting, the dreams stopped.

LETTING GO OF STRESS

This is a dream I seem to experience whenever I am stressed or anxious. I am in need of a bathroom and when I locate one the toilets are filthy and totally exposed, so there is no privacy. I feel embarrassed. Sometimes the stall is crowded with others. Sometimes I begin using the toilet and someone appears and sees me. The filth frightens me and I can't avoid touching it. I am frustrated because I need to relieve myself and can't under the circumstances.

Bathrooms, as we've discussed, represent cleansing and releasing. While the need to use the bathroom is a need to release something that no longer benefits you, for this dreamer there is a bit of a different spin—she feels embarrassed to relieve herself in front of others. Yet she has the dream when she is stressed and anxious, so she needs to let go of whatever is causing the stress and anxiety. She is also afraid of the filth that surrounds her, afraid that if she touches it she will become filthy as well. She feels that if she releases the excrement in her life she will appear dirty, and that others will judge her. So, whatever is frustrating her, she ends up keeping it inside. She wants a private place to get it out of her system.

It would seem that the dreamer feels guilty about letting go of stress and doesn't want to be perceived as bad for doing so. Someone who might have this type of dream is a mother of several young children. She loves her children, without a doubt, but they are still the source of much of her stress and anxiety. If she wants a little time away, even just time for a walk or a bubble bath, she feels guilty. What if the children need her? What will others think of her for hiring a babysitter just so that she can have a pedicure? She is tormented by stress, and can't relieve herself because it could make her seem like a self-indulgent person or a bad mother.

Since she keeps having this dream, I think she might benefit from having a session with a therapist. Therapists don't judge people and, by listening objectively as she releases whatever it is inside, perhaps the therapist can offer positive suggestions. Then, maybe the dreamer will finally feel relieved.

ANOTHER WOMAN'S STORY

I have had versions of toilet and bathroom dreams all my life. However, for about a year, I have been in therapy, uncovering the awful facts of my childhood sexual abuse. For some reason, I didn't connect the dream to my experiences. Now, I can't see how I missed it! Maybe I'll be able to let go of the bad stuff and flush it. The last time I had the dream, there was a door on the stall. It had had openings in it, so it's a start!

A lifetime of bathroom dreams finally made sense when this dreamer discovered what it was she needed to cleanse from her life. This woman has determined the meaning of her own dreams expertly and, as she continues to process her past in therapy, there is no doubt the dreams will stop.

A TOILET DREAM SUCCESS STORY

I had been plagued with a toilet dream three to four times a month for eight years. However, I haven't had the dream in two months. Two months ago, I stopped being bulimic, a compulsion to binge, then purge in the nearest bathroom, no matter where. Even though I found it disgust-

*ing, until now my bulimia was the thing in my life I couldn't release.
Therapy helped me to understand and overcome bulimia. Now I understand what my dreams were trying to communicate.*

The two-month absence of the bathroom dream is the strongest
clue that this dreamer is on track. Paying attention to the connection between the timing of events in her life and what she is dreaming about can help in understanding their hidden meanings.

SHOWERING IN YOUR DREAMS

*In my recurring dream, I am in a shower. The exact environment
changes, but the activity is the same. I am desperately trying to get soap
out of my hair and off my body! Usually, in the dream there is not
enough water coming out of the shower but, for whatever reason, I can
never get rid of all the soap.*

The first question this dreamer needs to ask is how would she feel if
she actually were lathered up in soap and she couldn't rinse it off?
That feeling may offer clues as to the meaning of her dream.

On the level of symbols and associations, soap is used for
cleansing. Hair is associated with strength, as in the Biblical story
of Samson, who lost his strength when his hair was cut. Hair is also
connected with sexuality, virility, seduction, health, and power.
Water is associated with cleansing, and also with emotions and the
unconscious, or that which is unknown to the dreamer. She can't
rinse, which is the completion of the cleansing process, so the job is
unfinished. She should ask herself what needs to be cleansed from
her life? What has she started to clean up and hasn't finished? Since
there is never enough water, perhaps this is an emotional issue that
needs to be cleansed.

A s k   Y o u r s e l f

Our dreams can reveal our state of health—emotionally, mentally,
spiritually and physically. Whenever you have a recurring dream, it

is a message from your unconscious mind asking you to pay attention to something. If you dream of bathrooms or, specifically, toilets ask yourself:

- What do I need to eliminate from my life?
- What is my fear connected to making this change?
- What can I let go of to feel relieved?
- Is a cleansing in order?
- What would I love to wash away?

The answers to these questions should put you in touch with the source of the problem. If you feel that you need assistance, please do not hesitate to seek professional guidance. Dreams can be the indication of stress or trauma that we don't recognize in our waking state. Especially when a dream is recurring, it is a sign that we should get to the bottom of the meaning and seek a remedy if required.

CHAPTER THIRTY-ONE

Spiritual Guidance in Your Dreams

D*reams have played a major role in the genesis* of many of the world's religions. Through dreams, the religious founders were guided to create their doctrines and their movements. Believers regard these dreams as direct communications from God and the angels (although nonbelievers might suspect that the dreams are simply used to justify the leaders' own wishes).

※

THE ORIGINS OF THE KORAN

The Koran, the holy book of Islam, was given in a dream to the Prophet Mohammed, who attached great importance to dreams. Each morning, he and his disciples would share and interpret their dreams.

In the dream that began it all, Mohammed was approached by the Archangel Gabriel while camping near Mecca. Told to mount a mare named Elborak, he rode the horse to Jerusalem. There, in a temple, he met and prayed with Abraham, Moses, and Jesus. He mounted Elborak again and journeyed to the first heaven, where he was welcomed and was introduced to Adam, his father. Adam said, "Heaven is accomplishing your wishes, O my honored son, O greatest of prophets!"

Mohammed traveled through thirteen heavens and was greeted by all the great prophets of antiquity. At that point in the dream, he then passed through the Garden of Delights and visited the House of Adoration, a place where seventy thousand angels pay homage to God each day. The Almighty instructed Mohammed to pray fifty times a day. Moses, realizing how much time this would take, encouraged him to negotiate (sounds like Moses may have been one of the founders of William Morris!) and God finally agreed that five times a day was more practical. With this concession, Mohammed mounted Elborak and returned to the place in the desert where he began his journey.

Because this dream inspired the establishment of Islam, it has profoundly affected millions of people who follow the religion, just as the dreams of the Old Testament have influenced Judaism and Christianity.

*

TOM'S DREAM OF GOOD AND EVIL

I dreamed that I was in a high-rise building. There were some good people and two bad guys with guns. We had to use the stairs, because the elevator wasn't working. We were all climbing up and trying to avoid getting hurt by the bad guys. I was trying to figure out how to get their guns away from them. We kept moving up. Then, a big bear began attacking one of the bad guys. His gun fell to the ground and I was able to get it. The bear was kind of mauling and eating the bad guys, but some good people got hurt, too. All the while, we continued to climb the stairs.

This is the dream of a young man in the process of investigating different philosophies and rethinking his spiritual values. Raised in a fundamentalist Christian home, Tom read the Bible three times from cover to cover before he was twenty-five. The dream is an indication of his spiritual growth (moving upward). As he continues to go upward, one step at a time, he is confronted with good and evil. The bear may be a symbol of deep inner truth, for it reaches deep into the tree looking for honey. This dream, then, suggests that the truth will overtake evil or wrong beliefs. The guns here represent the negative judgment of others as Tom decides for himself what he truly believes. Even good people can be hurt by blind acceptance of dogma.

This is a reassuring dream, encouraging the dreamer to continue his exploration and quest. Despite the judgments or opposition of others, he will recognize right from wrong and will continue to grow or move upward.

A MAJOR LIFE TRANSITION

I was driving my Mercedes convertible with the top down. It was a lovely afternoon. I was only a few blocks from home, when I came to an intersection. The light was red, so I stopped. I was the first but not the only car at the light. As I sat waiting for the light to turn green, I noticed someone standing in the middle of the intersection. It was someone that I knew from work. His name was Joe, the same as mine.

At the television station where we both worked, I was a director, he was the sports anchor. He looked disoriented and confused. I got out of my car, leaving the door open and walked to where he was standing. I asked if he was okay. He didn't answer. I was concerned for his well-being. I asked him again, but still he wouldn't or couldn't answer. I told him that everything would be all right, that we could walk to my house and shoot some hoops. I had a basketball hoop in my driveway. I put my arm around him and we started off, me leading him up the steep hill that lead to my house. It occurred to me briefly that I was leaving my favorite car behind.

In real life, I collected and restored antique cars and trucks. I had also collected a number of other possessions including two boats, two houses, and a motorcycle. In the house in which I lived, I had an elaborate shop setup with every possible tool. Of all of it, I think that little Mercedes convertible was my favorite. So, in my dream I had a moment of recogni-

tion that I was leaving my car running with the keys in it, the door open standing in the middle of the street, and that I might never see it again. My concern for Joe was greater.

We climbed the steep hill without much effort, and arrived at my house. We walked down the drive and entered the garage shop. Again, I was leading the way, reassuring Joe that everything was going to be fine. I noticed right away that everything in the shop had been moved and pushed to one side. The door to the house was open, and as I approached the door a man came out.

I was on guard, and asked him what the hell he was doing there in my house moving my stuff. He response was measured and calm. He said that he lived there now. I was suspicious. "What do you mean?" Again, with equal calm he stated that he lived there now. I asked who he was. He said his name was Joe. I was a little angry; I asked him again how he came to live in my house. His reply was that I was dead and that he lived there now. I challenged him with what I already knew to be true, "And that means that you get my house and all of my stuff and my girl-friend?" His reply was a simple nod, yes. "How did I die?" I demanded. He said it was a virus. "And, just like that, you take over all of my stuff." Again, he nodded yes. I turned to the other Joe standing in the driveway. He also nodded, yes, confirming that I was dead. Suddenly, my concern for the original Joe returned. He still had not spoken to me. I went to where he stood and put my arm around his shoulder. I realized that he too, was dead; it was new to him and that explained his confusion and si-lence. I once again began to console and comfort. I started to explain just how great it was going to be now that we were dead. We started walking away from the house, back down the steep hill. I was explaining that we no longer would have any needs. We never have to pay any bills and we could never get sick. As I was telling him this, we left the steep road. We were no longer walking down—we walked straight off into the sky leav-ing everything below.

Then, I woke up. I remembered in perfect detail the entire dream I just had. I was surprised that I didn't feel the slightest concern. Rather, I was filled with a contentment and tranquility like I had never experi-enced. I lay there for some time relaxed, taking in and recalling the dream. I felt so at peace. I hadn't felt this good in quite a while.

Two weeks later I was offered a job in another city. Within a month, I would move across the country, leaving everything I had behind. I didn't know it yet, but I was about to meet the most amazing woman in the world, and she became my girlfriend.

This dream is a precognitive warning, preparing the dreamer for a major transformation in his life. Prior to having the dream, Joe was feeling pressured by his life, especially by all the things in his life. He was stressed and wondering how to simplify things and still keep what he wanted. The financial obligations he was responsible for were causing sleepless nights.

The three men in his dream were all named Joe. Even though they were different people, including one he actually knew, they all represented certain aspects of himself. He was there, driving his favorite car. Cars and all vehicles in a dream can represent our bodies, since the physical body is the vehicle for the mind and spirit. Driving the car means that he is in charge, as opposed to being a passenger and leaving the choices up to someone else. Along his life path he gets stopped at a red light, a symbol everyone understands, and he leaves his car behind (a sign of giving up the life he knew). Here, the car represents a favorite material possession as well.

The Joe in the intersection represents the dreamer at a crossroad in his life. He could go in any direction from where he is. This Joe happens to be a very successful, nice-looking, popular guy from work. The dreamer recognizes these same qualities in himself. But this Joe can not communicate, he is disoriented; very possibly this is a reflection of the unconscious state of mind of the dreamer. So, the conscious or aware part of Joe easily leaves behind his favorite material possession to take care of the vulnerable, unconscious part of himself. He sees that his mental health is a priority over collecting material things—even really cool things.

The two men walk up a hill to the house. Up is generally a good thing in dreams; it indicates moving toward one's goals. But, here, the path is steep, a sign that it is a tough or challenging situation. The suggestion to shoot some hoops may have been a reference to the second Joe being a sports reporter, but playing a game in a dream often refers to playing the game of life. (What move should I make? What will be the outcome? Will I win or lose?) When they arrive at the home, once again, we deal with the accumulation of material goods. Someone has moved Joe's stuff—in fact he has moved into the home. Who is it? Joe number three!

The dreamer is told that he died of a virus. At face value, this would be quite disturbing. This, like most dreams, is not a literal depiction. Death in the symbolic language of dreams most often indicates a transition, a metamorphosis, something major changing. One thing ends or dies to allow for the new thing or new beginning. The word *virus* could scare you into believing that you were going to get sick. This is as far from the truth as possible. Dream symbols are often bold; so that you will remember them, they need to stand out. You must ask yourself what this represents to you. When you encounter a symbol in a dream and do not understand its meaning in the context of your dream, try looking up the word in a standard dictionary. *Virus*, according to *Webster's New World Dictionary*'s third definition, is "Anything that corrupts or poisons the mind or character." A virus is also capable of multiplying. *Influenza*, commonly know as the flu, is caused by a virus.

So, a virus is a bug of sorts, and the responsibility of owning and trying to pay for all these material things was certainly bugging Joe. The stress was beginning to poison his mind, in the sense that he was no longer happy and not able to really enjoy all the things he was working so hard to afford. Since in the dream he even loses his girlfriend when he "dies," Joe may believe that, without the material trappings, he won't be able to have a woman in his life. When Joe the dreamer accepts that the materialistic part of his life is over, he again considers the well-being of his mental state, represented by Joe the sports guy. As they walk down the hill, things get easier. He talks of the benefits, including paying no bills. The two then walk off into the sky. The sky is the limit when this dreamer gets his priorities straight and releases the burdens that dragged him down.

Joe did leave behind his "stuff," he was offered a wonderful job opportunity, and has moved up the corporate ladder. In the five years since this dream, Joe has lived in a small but comfortable apartment in New York City. He has not lacked for love; in fact he met a lovely woman who became his girlfriend. She earned at least as much money as he did so money was not an issue in their relationship. He learned that he didn't have to have a lot of material possessions to attract love.

The peaceful feeling that remained with Joe after waking from the dream was a clue as to how he would feel once he had actually made the transition. Dreams can truly help us to see and accept change. They can offer advice for our well-being and can predict our future.

MY OWN SPIRITUAL GUIDANCE

Several years ago I had a wonderfully spiritual dream that concluded and resolved a lifelong fear and opened my eyes to a profound spiritual truth. My first memory of swimming was at age five, when my family was invited to visit the home of my dad's boss. My four siblings and I were in the pool with my parents at the same time. Since I am the oldest and my parents had triplets under the age of two, no one was watching me and I got in over my head. Even though my mother didn't see me go under, her instinct saved the day, and she pulled me out of the water in time. It all happened so fast! I remember the burning in my nose and that I had swallowed some water. I was very relieved to sit on the edge and watch for the rest of the day.

Years later, when I was twelve, I was visiting relatives on the Lake of the Ozarks in Missouri. While walking along a floating bridge that led to a fishing dock, once again I fell in over my head. I did not know how to swim, but I remember being well under the surface and trying to simulate a swimming stroke; all the while it was quiet and surreal. I wondered if I would get into trouble. I wondered if I would lose my eyeglasses. I was very frightened, but in a weird way I felt calm in the murky water. My great-uncle must have run like lightning from up the hill near the house in time to pull me out of the lake. Once again, it was a pretty big deal. At family reunions they'll say, "Do you remember when you nearly drowned in the lake?" I recall sitting in a tire swing and contemplating the meaning of life for a long while after that experience.

As an adult, I finally felt it was time to face my fear and learn to swim. It took a while and my fear was intense. My very patient boyfriend taught me the basics. Soon after, we took a vacation to Maui, Hawaii. It was time to take the next step and learn to snorkel. I realized that I had always thought of the ocean as a surface, never considering the amazing and beautiful world below, until I actually had the snorkeling mask on. Then, just by tilting my face down below the surface, I could see the mysterious world below. I even fed frozen peas to the colorful fish! This was one of the most personally satisfying and delightful days of my life; I had beaten my fear and discovered a whole new amazing world.

That night I had a wonderfully beautiful and significant dream.

I was in an airport at gate seven. Just as I could tilt my masked face below the surface of the water and see the world of the ocean, so was I told that if I were to tilt my face upward, I would see the beautiful and amazing spirit world. There around me were lovely spirits and angels. They had been there all along, but I hadn't looked for them.

The spiritual dimension of this dream is clear, but the details are interesting, too. The airport is associated with air travel and the number seven with spiritual matters. My encounter with a world I was unaware of, that had indeed always existed below the sea, made me ready to receive this dream's powerful spiritual assurance that we are never alone. The message of the dream for me was that spiritual beings and angels don't live way up in the sky somewhere, as I had believed when I was a child, but that they are always all around us.

THE FIRST HINT that you have had a spiritual dream is your feeling about the dream. You can also look for symbols such as angels, Buddha, Jesus, the Virgin Mary, Gandhi, or other spiritual figures. Some dreamers have seen Merlin the Magician from the King

Arthur myths; Yoda, the wise character from the *Star Wars* movies; Jimminy Cricket, the character who represents the conscience in *Pinocchio;* and other images representing wisdom and guidance in spiritual dreams.

Dreams of spiritual guidance always feel magical and special. Record them in your journal, so that you can review them when you desire spiritual consolation and comfort. Dreams of spiritual guidance may relate directly to our religious or spiritual lives or they can offer what may be divine guidance for our everyday concerns and decisions. Like an answered prayer, they are available to every dreamer who opens his or her heart and mind to them.

Conclusion

Are you in earnest? Seize this very minute: What you can
do, or dream you can, begin it; Boldness has genius, power
and magic in it. Only begin and then the mind grows
heated; begin and the work will be completed.

— GOETHE

What would you like to change at this moment? What shift would make your life better, more fulfilling, or happier? Even the most content person has a next goal—what is yours?

Everything we do begins with a thought, but some of our thinking is below the surface, dwelling in our subconscious minds. Even though we are not aware of these thoughts, they direct our lives, and sometimes they take us in directions we're not conscious we want to go.

Your dreams are a method of bringing those hidden thoughts into focus. Once you understand what they are, you have the power of choice. You become the master of your destiny. As we have seen in the previous pages, dreams can offer assistance and guidance in all areas of our lives: relationships, career, health, and spirituality. If you fear knowing the underlying thoughts that motivate your behavior and moods, you are essentially giving away the keys to your life.

According to the Kaballah, "When the student is ready to learn, the teacher will appear." The following dream is a superb example of a man who, as an adult, remembered a recurring nightmare that he experienced for many years as a child. The dream came back into his conscious memory at a time in his life when he was ready to understand its meaning. The result of the understanding gave him tremendous insight into his pattern of choosing the wrong romantic partners, and it presented him with an opportunity to learn, grow, and make changes that could enhance the rest of his life by allowing him to open his heart to true love.

DELIVERING THE MILK

I am in my forties now, but I had this dream many times between the ages of nine and fourteen. I am delivering milk, but it is on my actual paper route. One guy wants me to put the two glass milk bottles just inside the kitchen door, so I go up to his house and the door is slightly open. I go to put the milk holder down and I look into the room. A man is tied up in a chair and two thugs are there with him. They see me and I look away as if to communicate—I don't see a thing, you just go on about your business, but they make me come in. I glance around and realize that now we are on a very high floor of the building, I can't just jump out the window. The bad guys get a vacuum cleaner and put the hose into the mouth of the man in the chair. They reverse the airflow so the guy is blowing up like a balloon. It never occurs to me to help him in any way. Pretty soon, he explodes, and I have blood and guts all over my shirt. The bad guys come back for me, and before they can grab me I decide to take my chances and jump off the balcony. To my amazement, I drop and roll, and I survive!

During this same period of my life, my mother was married to an abusive man. I would overhear yelling and screaming and I knew that she was being beaten. I felt impotent to do anything to help her, and guess I just tried to survive myself.

It wasn't until recently that I understood a deeper meaning of this dream. I have never married, although I like the idea of finding the one woman who would rock my world one thousand percent, the woman I absolutely wouldn't want to live without. However, nearly all of the women I have dated have needed me in some major way. It seems I have made a romantic career out of saving, helping, and protecting women. Then, when they get on their feet or resolve their particular situation, I don't feel needed any more and I move on. I never let myself get too close because I know that nothing lasts forever. The thing is that my mom has been in a happy and healthy relationship now for the past twenty years, and I am still playing out this scenario! I wonder now how this awareness will affect my future relationships.

This dreamer is interpreting a childhood dream to understand a lifelong unconscious pattern. The details of the dream are revealing, starting with milk, our first food. This man has continued to deliver nourishment and assistance to women in an effort to help and protect his mother. He has unconsciously been trying to make up to his mother for what he could not do as a child. In the dream, the man tied to the chair is him, a symbolic representation of how his hands were tied in trying to protect his mother. The bad guys, of course, represent the abusive stepfather—(there may as well have been two of them, for this little boy could not fight them; he would have been overpowered). He was blowing up inside, and the blood and guts represent how emotionally upsetting the effect of the abuse was on him. Being aware of the blood on him also reflects the guilt he felt at not being able to help or protect his mother. When he jumped out, which in his actual life he did by joining the Coast Guard, he survived.

Now, his task is to understand that he does not have to save anyone but himself. If he can accomplish this, and it would seem that he is well on his way, he will be able to have a mutually loving relationship. He should be able to let a woman into his heart on a deeper level than ever before. It took over thirty years from the time the recurring dream began for him to realize this, but it is never too late to turn around an old pattern and create a happy and healthy life.

Dreams can help us in other ways as well. Besides personal awareness, they can inspire our creativity. Many creative people use the inspiration of their dreams to write novels and songs, create paintings and sculpture, or as a seed to create wealth. Others have found healing or protective warnings through their dreams.

The great news is that your dreams come to you every night, free of charge. All you need to do is follow the simple steps outlined here to begin remembering and understanding them. If you fear what you will find, or want help in healing from these realizations, there are wonderful dream groups and therapists who can assist you. Remember that knowledge is power, and the power is in your hands. Having the life you want is as close as your pillow!

Bibliography

Allenbaugh, Eric. *Wake-Up Calls: You Don't Have to Sleepwalk Through Your Life, Love or Career!* New York: Fireside, 1992.

Behr, C. A. *Aelius Aristides and the Sacred Tales.* Amsterdam: Adolf M. Hakkert, 1968.

Brighmam, Deirdre Davis with Adelaide Davis and Derry Cameron-Sampey. *Imagery for Getting Well: Clinical Applications of Behaviorial Medicine.* New York: W. W. Norton & Company, 1994.

Brunton, Paul. *The Wisdom of the Overself.* New York: E. P. Dutton, 1946.

Castaneda, Carlos. *The Art of Dreaming.* New York: HarperCollins, 1994.

Hall, James. *Symbols in Eastern and Western Art.* London: John Murray Publishers, 1994.

Hall, Manly. "The Dream State." *Horizon Magazine, Journal of the Philosophical Research* (Summer 1946): 1–30.

———. *Dream Symbolism.* Los Angeles, California: The Philosophical Research Society, 1965.

Jung, Carl G. *Flying Saucers: A Modern Myth of Things Seen in the Skies.* Princeton, New Jersey: Princeton University Press, 1978.

———. *Man and His Symbols.* New York: Doubleday, 1964.

———. *Memories, Dreams Reflections.* New York: Vintage Books, 1989.

Kast, Verena. *The Dynamics of Symbols: Fundamentals of Jungian Psychotherapy.* New York: Fromm International Publishing, 1992.

Kübler-Ross, Elisabeth, M.D. *On Death and Dying.* New York: Scribner, 1997.

Linn, Denise. *Past Lives, Present Dreams.* New York: Ballantine Books, 1994.

MacLaine, Shirley. *Going Within.* New York: Bantam Books, 1989.

———. *Out on a Limb.* New York: Bantam Books, 1983.

Matheson, Richard. *What Dreams May Come.* New York: Tom Doherty Associates, 1978.

Paracelsus. *Selected Writings.* Edited by Jolande Jacobi. Translated by Norbert Guterman. Princeton, New Jersey: Princeton University Press, 1995.

Steiner, Rudolf. *How to Know Higher Worlds: A Modern Path of Initiation.* Translated by Christopher Bamford. Anthroposophic Press, 1994.

Talbot, Michael. *The Holographic Universe.* New York: HarperCollins, 1991.

Vaughan-Lee, Llewellyn. "Dreams and the Sufi Path." *Gnosis, A Journal of the Western Inner Traditions* (Winter 1992): 48–50.

Vogel, Virgil J. *American Indian Medicine.* Oklahoma: University of Oklahoma Press, 1990.

Yoganananda, Paramahansa. *Autobiography of a Yogi.* Los Angeles, California: Self-Realization Fellowship, 1988.

Walter, Katya. *Tao of Chaos: DNA and the I Ching, Unlocking the Code of the Universe.* Brisbane, Australia: Element Publishers, 1994.

I n d e x